David Beaton was educated at Quainton Hall, Ardingly College and St. Andrews University. He is married with two children and lives in Gillingham, having retired from teaching in 2002. His time is now spent making music, playing golf, reading, gardening, going to the theatre, researching his writing, and sharing the endless beauty and variety of Dorset with his London-based grand-children. *Dorset's Forgotten Heroes* is his second book. His first, *Dorset Maps*, was published by The Dovecote Press in 2001. He has lived in Dorset for the past 28 years.

DORSET'S
Forgotten Heroes

DAVID BEATON

THE DOVECOTE PRESS

First published in 2005 by
The Dovecote Press Ltd
Stanbridge, Wimborne Minster, Dorset BH21 4JD

ISBN 1 874336 99 7

© David Beaton 2005

Printed and bound in Singapore

All papers used by The Dovecote Press are natural, recyclable products
made from wood grown in sustainable, well-managed forests.

A CIP catalogue record for this book is available
from the British Library

1 3 5 7 9 8 6 4 2

Contents

Introduction

Inevitably a book of this nature calls into question the definition of the word hero. Must it be someone who has done a courageous act? My own feeling is that it needs to be broader than that, to include those who have been selfless in their service to others (such as the Reverend Sidney Osborne, champion of the rural poor in Victorian England), or dedicated in their chosen field (such as Mary Anning and her significant role in early palaeontology), or those who have discovered a miracle cure (such as Benjamin Jesty, the first known person to have practised vaccination against smallpox, which has saved literally millions of lives).

Thus this book covers a wide range of people, some of whom are still living, some of whom have only recently died, some of whom lived only a generation or two ago, and some of whom are lost in the mists of time. In many cases their name lives on, but if their story is forgotten, they have found their way into these pages. In a few cases their achievements are so well documented that they have been omitted, such as author Thomas Hardy, poet William Barnes and pioneer photographer William Henry Fox Talbot (born at Melbury Sampford in 1800).

What they all have in common, however, is a story which is inspirational and which will linger in the memory. Before the general populace was able to read and write, the stories of the lives of such people were handed down orally from one generation to the next, and there was a collective memory that ensured that they were not forgotten.

It seems strange that advances in education have tended to lead to deterioration in memory skills, but we lose our sense of historical perspective at our peril. People who have no past have no future, and a book such as this is intended to shed light on the people who have made Dorset what it is, and to provide inspiration for present and future inhabitants of the county.

Acknowledgements

I am grateful to the following for their help. Tony and Pam Baker, for suggesting Dodo Lees and for putting me in touch with Commander Selby Bennett; Sally Beaton, my wife, for her patient proof-reading; Charles Boldero, for material relating to George Stainforth; James Chandler, whose fascinating book *Great Characters in Dorset* has been a fine introduction to several heroes who would not otherwise have found their way into these pages; Barry Cox, Hon Librarian RNLI, for allowing to use information and illustrations from *Lifeboat Gallantry;* Roger Guttridge, for the photograph of Charles Bennett, his invaluable assistance and for publicising my quest for material; Dr Richard Hall, for suggesting Sir Dan Godfrey; David and Geraldine Hobson, for information about Violet Cross; Felicity Herring, for useful historical information; Betty Hockey, for information about Southern Command Concert Party; Douglas Jackson, for help with Violet Cross; Peter James, for his suggestions and book loan; Chris Jervis, for putting me on to Mark Rathbone; Colin Kingman, for material relating to James Knight, VC; Steve Lee, for supplying material relating to Dorset's VCs; Bill Loud, for information about himself and for the loan of books; Eric Marsh, for suggestions of heroes from Poole; Philip Mitchell, for information about Violet Cross; Nick O'Hara, for help with Wimborne Town Football Club; Kenneth Oxford, for suggesting heroes from Bournemouth and Poole; Rodney Pattisson, for information about himself and his father, Lt-Cdr Kenneth Pattisson; Mark Rathbone, for help with Lady Charlotte Guest and Lady Wimborne; Harry Riggs, for material relating to James Knight, VC; Commander 'Chipps' Selby Bennett, for information about Dodo and Michael Lees; Ted Ware, for material about Sidney Ware, VC; Joe West, for information about Robert Montague Poore and for suggesting Alfred Russel Wallace; David White, for information about Violet Cross; Marjorie Winzar, for supplying material about Ann Winzer.

ONE

Supreme Courage

There are 35 VCs with a Dorset connection, but as some of those are tenuously linked, only those with a strong link to the county will be included.

This chapter tells the stories of all ten Dorset-born men awarded the Victoria Cross, the one Dorsetshire Regiment VC, and some of the VCs who spent (or in Jack Mantle's case, lost) their lives in Dorset.

The award was created in 1856 at the time of the Crimean War, and the first sixty-two VCs were presented in June 1857, at a review in Hyde Park, by Queen Victoria, seen on horseback for the first time in public.

The Queen had taken a great interest in her new award, especially in the design of the Cross. When the first drawings were submitted, she selected one closely modelled on an existing campaign medal, the Army Gold Cross from the Peninsular War, suggesting only that it should be 'a little smaller'. She also made a significant alteration to the motto, striking out 'FOR THE BRAVE' and substituting 'FOR VALOUR', in case anyone should come to the conclusion that the only brave men in a battle were those who won the Cross.

The Victoria Cross is the highest and most prestigious award for gallantry in the face of the enemy, awarded (almost without exception) to members of the British and Commonwealth armed forces. A case of the award going to a recipient outside these forces was when the British Government conferred a VC on the Unknown US Soldier in Arlington Cemetery, Virginia.

To date 1,355 Victoria Crosses have been awarded.

Crimean War

Joseph Kellaway (1824-1880)

Born on 1 September 1824 at Kingston on the Isle of Purbeck, Joseph Kellaway was 30 when he earned his VC. As a Boatswain on HMS *Wrangler* in the Sea of Azov, Crimea, Kellaway was put ashore with the mate and three seamen to burn some boats, fishing stations and haystacks on the other side of a small lake. They had nearly reached the spot when they were ambushed by fifty Russians.

One of the men fell into Russian hands, and Kellaway and the two other seamen were making their escape, when the mate accidentally fell. Kellaway immediately returned to help him, but the two were quickly surrounded, and notwithstanding a gallant resistance by Kellaway, he and the mate were taken prisoner.

He was later promoted to Chief Boatswain. His grave is at Maidstone Road Cemetery, Chatham. His VC is not publicly held.

Henry Raby (1827-1907)

Educated at Sherborne School, Lieutenant (later Rear-Admiral) Henry James Raby, RN, Naval Brigade, became the first person to receive the Victoria Cross, in the first investiture at Hyde Park in 1857.

The story goes that the Queen, leaning forward from her side-saddle position on her horse, in her eagerness to make sure that the medal was properly attached, pinned it through the flesh on Raby's chest beneath his uniform. The Lieutenant received his award unflinchingly, the incident no doubt paling into insignificance by comparison with the action that earned him his VC.

On 18 June 1855 in the Crimea, immediately after the assault on Sebastopol, a soldier of the 57th Regiment, who had been wounded in both legs, was observed sitting up and calling for help.

At once Raby and two seamen left the shelter of their battery works and ran forward 70 yards across open ground, through heavy gunfire, and succeeded in carrying the wounded man to safety. For this action all three men were awarded the VC.

Raby's grave is at the Highland Road Cemetery in Portsmouth, where his VC is on display at the Royal Naval Museum.

Indian Mutiny

Philip Salkeld (1830-1857)

Philip Salkeld was born on 13 October 1830 in Fontmell Magna, where his father was rector. When he was 26, he earned his VC for his action at Delhi during the Indian Mutiny, while a Lieutenant in The Bengal Engineers.

With another Lieutenant, a Sergeant and a Bugler he showed conspicuous gallantry in the desperate task of blowing in the Kashmir Gate in broad daylight under heavy and destructive musket fire, preparatory to the assault. All four were awarded the Victoria Cross.

Salkeld was killed in action in Delhi just under a month later. His remains are in an unmarked grave in the Old Delhi Cemetery, although he has a fine memorial cross in St Andrew's Churchyard, Fontmell Magna. There is also a bridge to Salkeld's memory near to the entrance to Plumber Manor, on the outskirts of Hazelbury Bryan. On either side of the road the stone parapet reads simply: 'Salkeld – 1857 – Delhi'. His VC is not publicly held.

William Bankes (1836-1858)

William George Hawtry Bankes of Kingston Lacy was born on 11 September 1836. He was 21 years old and a Cornet in the 7th Hussars (The Queen's Own), when he earned his VC for his action during the Indian Mutiny.

On 19 March 1858 at Lucknow, Cornet Bankes led three charges against a body of fanatical rebels who had rushed the guns in the vicinity of Moosa-Bagh. In the course of these charges the young officer was almost cut to pieces.

He died of his wounds eighteen days later and is buried in an unknown grave in Lucknow. His VC is displayed at the Queen's Own Hussars Museum in Warwick.

Shimonoseki Expedition

Thomas Pride (1835-1893)

Born in Wareham on 29 March 1835, Thomas Pride earned his VC at the age of 29, while serving in the Royal Navy during the Shimonoseki Expedition, Japan.

On 6 September 1864 Pride was one of the two Colour Sergeants who accompanied the midshipman from HMS *Euryalus*, when they carried the Queen's Colour into action in the capture of the enemy's stockade.

They kept the flag flying in spite of the fierce fire which killed the other Colour Sergeant and severely wounded Pride. He and the midshipman, however, did not falter and were only finally prevented from going further forward by direct orders from their superior officer.

Pride lived on in Dorset to the age of 58 and is buried in All Saint's Churchyard, Branksome Park. His VC is displayed at the National Maritime Museum in Greenwich.

Indian Campaign

Samuel Vickery (1873-1952)

Born at Wambrook, Somerset, in February 1873, Samuel Vickery joined up as a Private in the 1st Battalion, The Dorsetshire Regiment, and was 24 years old when he fought in the Tirah Campaign, India.

In October 1897, during the attack on the Dargai Heights, Vickery ran down the slope and rescued a wounded comrade under heavy fire, bringing him back to cover. He went on to distinguish himself in a subsequent action, killing three of the enemy who attacked him when he was separated from his company.

He later achieved the rank of Corporal, and lived on to the ripe old age of 79, dying in June 1952. His grave is at the Glyntaff Crematorium, Pontypridd, Mid-Glamorgan. His VC can be seen at the Keep Military Museum in Dorchester.

Boer War

James Knight (1878-1955)

At the start of the twentieth century it was a rare distinction for a regiment to have in its ranks three VCs serving simultaneously, but such was the proud boast of The King's (Liverpool) Regiment. Even rarer was the timescale in which the VCs were won – three medals in three days.

One of those was James Huntley Knight, who was born in Yeovil in 1878, but spent his childhood in Dorset, initially in Poole and then in Milborne St Andrew.

He earned his VC in the Boer War while a Corporal in the 1st Battalion, The King's (Liverpool) Regiment. From the time of the siege of Ladysmith in January 1900 to August, the 4th Division took part in the advance to Natal and the Eastern Transvaal, and was almost continuously engaged with the enemy.

On 21 August, during the operations near Van Wyk's Vlei, Knight's unit was surrounded by a superior force of Boers, and a part of it was only able to withdraw from the position through the cool and gallant conduct of Knight and a fellow Sergeant, both of whom were awarded the Victoria Cross.

Knight's party consisted of himself and four men, who were covering the right rear of a detachment of their company when they were attacked by the enemy. The Corporal held his ground, directing his men to retire one by one to better cover, where he maintained his position for nearly an hour, delaying the advance of the Boers and allowing the complete company to withdraw to safety.

Meanwhile two of Knight's four soldiers were killed and the other two were wounded. He then retired, taking with him the two wounded, one of whom he carried back to camp, a distance of nearly two miles. Throughout this extraordinary act of extended bravery, the party were hotly engaged by the enemy.

Knight was immediately promoted to Sergeant, and in 1908 was promoted again. There followed an unusually varied army career, including temporary commissions of Lieutenant and Captain. Knight finally left the army in 1917, having served in Nova Scotia, Barbados, South Africa, India and France.

He returned to Milborne St Andrew, where he founded a branch of the Royal British Legion. Latterly, he lived in Winterborne Anderson, where he died in 1955. His ashes were scattered at Bournemouth Crematorium and his VC is on public display at The Museum of the King's Regiment, Liverpool. A headstone to his memory has been erected in Milborne St Andrew churchyard.

The First World War

Cecil Noble (1891-1915)

Cecil Reginald Noble was born on 4 June 1891 in Bournemouth. He was 23 and a Corporal in the 2nd Battalion, The Rifle Brigade (Prince Consort's Own), earning his VC in March 1915 at Neuve Chapelle.

When the advance of the battalion was impeded by wire entanglements and heavy machine-gun fire, Noble and another man voluntarily rushed forward and succeeded in cutting the wires. Both were wounded and Noble later died of his injuries.

For this action both men were awarded the Victoria Cross. Noble's grave is at Longuenesse Souvenir Cemetery, 2 miles south of Saint-Omer, France. His VC is not publicly held.

William Rhodes-Moorhouse (1887-1915)

Pioneer aviator William Barnard Rhodes-Moorhouse, of Parnham House, near Beaminster, put his name on the map of aviation history by being the first to fly under the Golden Gate Bridge in San Francisco. He was also the first to pilot passengers across the English Channel.

More lasting fame came when, aged 27, he earned his VC in an action on the Western Front which cost him his life, but gave the Royal Flying Corps (later the Royal Air Force) its first Victoria Cross.

Taking off from Merville, on 26 April 1915, in a BE-2b biplane, his orders were to drop a 100-pound bomb on a railway bridge, spanning the River Lys in German-occupied Belgium.

At 300 feet he flew into a heavy barrage of small arms fire from rifles and a machine-gun in the belfry of Courtrai church, but still succeeded in hitting his target and ripping up the railway track, even though he was severely wounded by a bullet in the thigh.

Returning to the Allied lines, Rhodes-Moorhouse again ran into heavy fire from the ground and was wounded twice more. He nevertheless managed to pilot his badly damaged plane back to Merville, and insisted on making his report before being taken to the Casualty Clearing Station, where he died the next day.

Posthumously he achieved what many others failed to achieve. He had requested that, in the event of his death, his body should be transported back to Dorset. His commanding officer was so impressed by the young Lieutenant's bravery that he granted this wish and additionally recommended him for a VC.

In 1914 Rhodes-Moorhouse's widow, Linda, had given birth to a baby son, William Henry, who followed in his father's footsteps in the next war, winning the DFC for 601 Squadron in the Battle of Britain. His Hurricane was shot down in 1940, near Tonbridge, Kent, while the battle was at its peak. William Henry's ashes were interred in the same Parnham plot with his father's remains. His mother's loss became a double tragedy, she having lost a husband and a son at the same age and in similar circumstances.

Sidney Ware (1892-1916)

Born the eldest of thirteen children on 11 November 1892 in Winterborne Whitechurch on the Whatcombe Estate, where his father was a dairyman, Sidney William Ware was 23 years old and a Corporal in the 1st Battalion, The Seaforth Highlanders, when he earned his VC for his action on 6 April 1916 at Sanna-i-Yat in Mesopotamia (now Iraq).

When an order was given to withdraw to a communication trench, Corporal Ware, whose cool gallantry had been marked during an advance, was one of the few men remaining unwounded. He picked up one of the wounded, carried him some 200 yards to cover, and then returned for others, moving to and fro under heavy fire for more than two hours until he had brought in all the wounded, and was completely exhausted.

He was killed in action in the Persian Gulf on 16 April 1916, just ten days later. Ware's grave is at the Amara War Cemetery, which may now be destroyed. His VC is on display at the Regimental Museum of The Queen's Own Highlanders at Fort George, Inverness-shire.

Jack Counter (1898-1970)

Jack Thomas Counter's remarkable story begins when he joined up in 1917, aged 18, in the 1st Battalion of the King's (Liverpool) Regiment. His moment of glory came just over a year later, on 16 April 1918, at Boisleux-Saint-Marc, six kilometres south of Arras in northern France.

On that fateful day the Battalion was faced with a breakthrough by the enemy, and vital information was needed from the front. 'The only way was from the support line along a sunken road and thence down a forward slope for about 250 yards with no cover, in full view of the enemy and swept by their machine-gun and rifle fire.' So reads the official report.

A detachment set out, but almost immediately one soldier was wounded and its leader killed. It was decided to send a solo runner, who would stand a better chance of going the distance. There was no shortage of volunteers – five times the dangerous passage was attempted and five times with fatal results.

The report continues: 'Private Counter, who had seen the five runners killed one after the other, then volunteered to carry the message. He went out under terrific fire and succeeded in getting through. He then returned, carrying with him the vital information with regard to the estimated number of enemy in our line, the exact position of our flank and the remaining strength of our troops. This information enabled his commanding officer to organise and launch the final counter-attack, which succeeded in regaining the whole of our position. Subsequently this man carried back five messages across the open under a heavy artillery barrage to company headquarters.'

The citation adds: 'Private Counter's extraordinary courage in facing almost certain death produced a most excellent impression on his young and untried companions.' The striking thing about this account is the immediacy of the style. The frequent use of the word 'our' indicates that the writer must be the commanding officer himself, probably writing up his notes in his dugout the very same evening.

The officer's inspiring citation led to Counter receiving the VC from King George V at Buckingham Palace on 22 June 1918, just two months later. He returned to Blandford to a hero's welcome and survived the rest of the war, settling in Jersey and working for the Post Office there.

In June 1920 the King invited recipients of the Victoria Cross to an Afternoon Party at Buckingham Palace, which Counter attended. He was subsequently promoted to Corporal and faithfully attended all further VC reunions in London, travelling each time from Jersey for the occasion.

Ironically, he ended his days in the town of his birth. On a return visit to Blandford in 1970, he was taken ill and died there, just two months short of his seventy-second birthday. He was cremated at Bournemouth and his ashes were interred beneath a headstone to his memory in St Saviour's Churchyard, St Helier.

The year after his death his image was used on a Jersey postage stamp and his VC is on display in Jersey Museum.

Frederick Riggs (1888-1918)

Born on 28 July in Bournemouth, Frederick Charles Riggs was 30 and a Sergeant in the 6th Battalion, The York and Lancaster Regiment, when his action at Epinoy on 1 October 1918 earned him his VC.

Having led his platoon through strong uncut wire under severe fire, he continued straight on and although losing casualties to heavy flanking fire, he succeeded in reaching his objective, where he captured a machine-gun.

Later he handled two captured guns with great effect and caused fifty of the enemy to surrender. Subsequently, when the enemy again advanced in force, Riggs cheerfully exhorted his men to resist to the last, and while doing so was killed.

He has no known grave, but his name is on the Vis-en-Artois Memorial in France. His VC is on public display in The York and Lancaster Regiment Museum at Rotherham in South Yorkshire. Riggs Gardens, Wallisdown, are named after him.

ABOVE Lieutenant Henry Raby carrying a wounded soldier to safety, after the assault on Sebastopol in the Crimean War. For this action he was awarded the Victoria Cross (see page 9).

ABOVE LEFT Corporal Cecil Noble, pictured here on a Gallaher cigarette card, was born in Bournemouth. He earned his VC in the First World War at Neuve Chapelle, when he volunteered to go forward and cut an entanglement of barbed wire that was impeding the advance of his battalion. (see page 13).

LEFT Corporal James Knight, pictured here on horseback, earned his VC in the Boer War in an extraordinary act of extended bravery (see page 12).

ABOVE LEFT Lieutenant William Rhodes-Moorhouse of Parnham House near Beaminster, was mortally wounded whilst bombing a railway bridge during the First World War. His Victoria Cross was the first to be awarded to a member of the Royal Flying Corps (later to become the RAF) (see page 13).

ABOVE RIGHT Corporal Sidney Ware was born on the Whatcombe Estate, and earned his VC for an action in April 1916 at Sanna-i-Yat in Mesopotamia (see page 14).

BELOW Lieutenant-Colonel Derek Seagrim's action in North Africa in 1943 led directly to the capture of an important objective, earning him his VC when he personally helped to place a scaling ladder over an anti-tank ditch and was the first across (see page 17).

ABOVE AND RIGHT Blandford-born Private Jack Counter was awarded his VC for his bravery in northern France in 1918. The photograph above shows him being honoured in Blandford after being presented with his VC by George V in London. A plaque to his memory can be seen on a house in Dorset Street.

He later settled in Jersey, working for the Post Office, which in 1971 issued the stamp on the right to commemorate the 50th anniversary of the British Legion (see page 15).

RIGHT Leading Seaman Jack Foreman Mantle earned his VC in July 1940. Firing his pom-pom gun from HMS *Foylebank* in Portland Harbour at German bombers, he continued firing after his leg was shattered by a bomb blast . Even after the ship's electrical systems had gone down, he continued to train and fire by hand until he collapsed and died at his post. He is buried in Portland Naval Cemetery (see page 17).

ABOVE LEFT Captain Henry Digby. The commemorative medal shows up the clearest in the portraits of the three Dorset Captains at Trafalgar. Digby's HMS *Africa* was the smallest ship in the battle, but engaged with the largest, the Spanish four-decker *Santissima Trinidada* (see page 22).

ABOVE Vice-Admiral Sir Charles Bullen. Like Hardy, Bullen is wearing his Trafalgar commemorative medal. This portrait gives very little hint of the dashing younger man whose HMS *Britannia* cut through the enemy lines shortly after the *Victory* (see page 20).

LEFT Captain Sir Thomas Masterman Hardy, Nelson's Captain on the *Victory* . This portrait was painted only four years after the Battle of Trafalgar, and Hardy can be seen wearing the commemorative medal. He was responsible for making sure that Lord Nelson's body was not buried at sea, but brought back for a state funeral at St. Paul's. Thousands of weeping people lined the route to the Cathedral (see page 19).

ABOVE Violet Cross of Hazelbury Bryan served as a nurse in both World Wars, narrowly escaping from France soon after the German occupation in 1940 (see page 26).

ABOVE RIGHT Wing-Commander Bill Loud, Spitfire ace, looking every inch the heroic airman. He won a DFC flying with 602 Squadron, and went on to command his own Wing, winning the Distinguished Service Order and a bar to his DFC (see page 29).

BELOW Lieutenant-Commander Kenneth Pattisson (centre), naval airman who flew a Swordfish in the heroic attack which put paid to the *Bismarck*'s career as an Atlantic commerce raider (see page 30).

6

ABOVE British airborne forces of the 6th Airborne Division at RAF Tarrant Rushton ready to take to the skies for the D-Day invasion landings. The troops who flew from Tarrant Rushton were amongst the first to set foot on French soil (see page 40).

OPPOSITE PAGE TOP LEFT Sub-Lieutenant Alasdair Ferguson, wartime RNVR officer who commanded landing craft at Dieppe and on D-Day (see page 32).

OPPOSITE PAGE TOP RIGHT Reg Hyde, a badly burned Second World War pilot who became a member of the 'Guinea Pig Club', a group of elite airmen who were treated by Sir Archibald McIndoe at his burns' unit in East Grinstead, Sussex. Plastic surgery was in its infancy and Hyde endured scores of pioneering operations to restore his face (see page 33).

OPPOSITE PAGE BOTTOM LEFT George Millar, an officer who served in the Special Operations Executive (SOE), formed on Winston Churchill's order to 'set Europe ablaze' after the fall of France in 1940. Millar was captured in North Africa, jumped from a German POW train near Munich and made his way back to Britain (see page 35).

OPPOSITE PAGE BOTTOM RIGHT Dodo Selby Bennett's colourful wartime career included working with the French Red Cross as an ambulance driver, living with the Maquis in the Vosges mountains and taking part in the liberation of Dachau concentration camp (see page 36) .

In 1940 Betty Hockey formed the Southern Command Concert Party, billed as the 'Nonstops Variety Troop Show'. By D-Day the Nonstops had given over a thousand performances to appreciative troops across the whole of the Southern Command area, contributing hugely to morale (see page 42).

The Second World War

Jack Mantle (1917-1940)

Jack Foreman Mantle, Leading Seaman, RN, was a Londoner, born in Wandsworth in 1917. Aboard HMS *Foylebank* at Portland, on 4 July 1940, he was manning the starboard 20mm pom-pom gun during an air raid, when his left leg was shattered by the blast from a bomb early in the action.

Although wounded time and again, he remained at his post, and when *Foylebank*'s electric power failed, he trained and fired by hand, until he collapsed and died.

His supreme courage is remembered annually on Portland – the outstanding sacrifice of a 23-year-old man dying on Dorset soil, while protecting his nation from enemy attack. His grave is in Portland Naval Cemetery. His VC, the first to be awarded for action in British Home Waters, is not publicly held.

Derek Seagrim (1903-1943)

Born on 24 September 1903 in Bournemouth, Derek Anthony Seagrim was 39 and a Lieutenant Colonel in the 7th Battalion, The Green Howards, when his action at the Mareth Line in Tunisia earned him his VC.

Colonel Seagrim's courage and leadership led directly to the capture of an important objective. When it appeared that the attack on the position would fail owing to the intensity of enemy fire, he placed himself at the head of his battalion and led them forward.

He personally helped to place a scaling ladder over an anti-tank ditch and was the first across. Leading an attack on two machine-gun posts, he accounted for twenty of the enemy and when a counter-attack was launched next day he moved from post to post quite unperturbed, until the counter-attack was defeated.

Seagrim was killed in action less than a month later, and his grave is at the Sfax Cemetery, Tunisia. His VC is not publicly held. Seagrim Road, Bournemouth, is named after him.

On 12 September 1946 Seagrim's brother, Hugh, who was born in 1909, was posthumously awarded the George Cross in 1946. He was executed by the Japanese after voluntarily surrendering to them in an attempt to stop them torturing the Burmese villagers who were helping him avoid capture.

After surrendering in March 1944 he was taken to Rangoon and, with eight others, was sentenced to death. He pleaded that only he should be executed, as the others had only obeyed his orders, but such was the devotion he had inspired in his men that they all elected to die with him, and they were duly executed on 22 September 1944 in Rangoon.

Derek and Hugh Seagrim remain the most highly decorated brothers in British military history, and are unique in the history of valour, being the only recipients of the Victoria Cross and George Cross in the same family.

Lionel Queripel (1920-1944)

Lionel Ernest Queripel was born on 13 July 1920 in Winterborne Monkton. He was a Captain in The Royal Sussex Regiment when, under heavy fire in September 1944 during the ill-fated attempt to hold a bridge over the Rhine at Arnhem, he carried a wounded sergeant to the regimental aid post and was himself wounded in the face. Later, when it became necessary to withdraw he insisted, despite the protests of his men, in remaining behind to cover their withdrawal, armed only with his pistol and a few hand grenades. This was the last occasion on which he was seen.

Queripel's grave is at the Arnhem Oosterbeek War Cemetery in The Netherlands. His VC is on public display at the Airborne Forces Museum at Aldershot, Hampshire.

TWO

Military Heroes

Napoleonic Wars

Thomas Masterman Hardy (1769-1939),
Nelson's Captain on the *Victory*

At Kingston Russell, near Long Bredy, a boy was born in 1769, and the die was cast for a great military career, for the boy, christened Thomas Masterman Hardy, was born in the same year as Wellington and Napoleon.

His maritime career began at the age of twelve when he went to sea as Captain's Servant on the brig *Helena*. After serving in the Merchant Service, Hardy joined the Royal Navy, becoming a Lieutenant by the age of twenty-one.

Hardy's role on *Victory* during the Battle of Trafalgar is well known, but it is not always realised that his close friendship with Nelson began some twelve years earlier in 1793.

In 1796 an incident occurred for which Nelson had good reason to be in Hardy's debt. Hardy was on board a ship that had been taken with a prize crew when Nelson's two small frigates were engaged by a superior Spanish squadron. Instantly realising the danger to Nelson, Hardy raised the English flag above the colours of his prize to draw the Spanish. He was overwhelmed and captured, but two months later was released in an exchange of prisoners and rejoined Nelson.

A measure of Nelson's regard for Hardy was shown soon afterwards. Nelson was being pursued by the Spanish fleet when an English sailor fell overboard. Hardy immediately put off in a boat to save the drowning man, while the Spaniards were fast overtaking Nelson's ship. Loath to abandon his friend, Nelson bellowed a command: 'I'll not lose Hardy; back the mizzen topsail.' The manoeuvre so surprised the Spanish fleet that they gave up the pursuit.

Hardy served with Nelson at the Battle of Cape St Vincent in 1797, he commanded the *Vanguard* at the Battle of the Nile in 1798 (where thirteen out of the seventeen French ships were destroyed), he took part in Nelson's mauling of the French fleet at Copenhagen in 1801, and he continued through to the dénouement of Admiral Villeneuve's 'cat and mouse' game of pursuit when, cornered and blockaded, Villeneuve gave battle to Nelson at Trafalgar.

Hardy brought his beloved Admiral's body home to a hero's funeral, and in 1806 was himself made a Baronet. He continued to hold naval commands for the rest of his life, eventually attaining the rank of Vice-Admiral, followed by his appointment to First Sea Lord and Governor of Greenwich Hospital.

Hardy died at Greenwich, aged seventy, in 1839. Five years after his death, in 1844, a memorial was erected at High Point on Black Down, above his home village of Portesham. The 70-foot high octagonal tower is visible far out to sea and is, fittingly, a landmark for mariners as well as being a monument to one of the great figures in naval history.

Charles Bullen (1768-1853),
Captain of the *Britannia* at the Battle of Trafalgar

Charles Bullen was the son of John Bullen of Weymouth, and it was there that he spent his childhood. Bullen's naval career began when he was just eleven years old, entering the service in 1779 as a first-class volunteer on the *Europe*, shortly afterwards being transferred to the sloop *Loyalist*, which took part in the fall of Charlestown during the American War of Independence, under the command of Admiral Marriott Arbuthnot.

Arbuthnot, too, was from Weymouth, and, being related to Bullen's father John, had used his influence to enable Charles to join the Navy. The Admiral, however, was criticised for his indecisive action at Chesapeake Bay in 1781, and was recalled to England, along with young Charles and his father, who was Surgeon-General on board.

Charles was promoted to Lieutenant in 1791, and was serving on the *Ramillies* when it saw action at Lord Howe's celebrated defeat of the French off Ushant at the Battle of the Glorious First of June, 1794.

Three years later, he showed his true mettle while serving on the *Monmouth* under the command of his Captain, the Earl of Northesk.

Bullen showed exceptional courage when he personally saved Lord Northesk from an angry mob during the Mutiny of the Nore. The Earl had been held prisoner on board his own ship, and the already difficult situation could have turned out considerably worse, but for Bullen's prompt action when, pistol in hand, he quickly drew a line on the deck, crying 'the first man who steps beyond this line, I'll shoot him dead.'

The mutiny was put down, and, later that year, now a First Lieutenant, he displayed great exertion and gallantry, after the Battle of Camperdown, by taking possession of the Dutch ship *Delft*, voluntarily staying aboard and saving many lives as the captured prize began to sink, being himself nearly drowned in the process. Twice a rescue boat took off wounded Dutch sailors, but before it could return a third time, the *Delft* foundered and sank to the bottom. Bullen jumped into the sea and was fortunately able to reach his own ship.

Bullen's rise through the ranks progressed inexorably. He was promoted to Commander after this incident, and was made a Captain in 1802. As Flag-Captain of the 100 gun *Britannia* under Lord Northesk at Trafalgar, Bullen's ship was amongst the first to engage the enemy. For this action he received the King's Trafalgar Gold Medal, the thanks of Parliament and a testimonial from the Lloyd's Patriotic Fund. His Trafalgar prize money amounted to over £3,000, the equivalent of £150,000 at today's value.

During the years 1807-11 he commanded successively the frigates *Volontaire* and *Cambrian* in the Mediterranean. Several dashing exploits enhanced his reputation when in 1809 he captured the island of Pomègues off Marseilles, and destroyed Fort Rioux near Cap de la Croisette.

He was Captain of the fifty-gun *Akbar* on the North American Station at Halifax from 1814-17, and was made a Companion of the Order of the Bath during this period. From 1824-27 Bullen was a Commodore serving on the west coast of Africa, where he liberated nearly 10,000 slaves. He was a Commissioner of Chatham Dockyard from 1831-32, and his final appointment was Superintendent of Pembroke Dockyard from 1832-37.

During this time he was also Captain of the yacht *Royal Sovereign*, and he received a knighthood in 1835. At the end of his Superintendency he was promoted to Rear-Admiral, then Vice-

Admiral in 1846, and Admiral of the Blue in 1852, the crowning achievement of his naval career.

Admiral Sir Charles Bullen died in Hampshire on 2 July 1853, aged 86, and is buried in St James's Churchyard, Shirley, near Southampton. His portrait hangs in the Painted Hall at Greenwich.

Henry Digby (1770-1842),
Captain of the *Africa* at the Battle of Trafalgar

Nephew of the 1st Earl of Digby and son of the Very Reverend the Honourable William Digby, Dean of Durham and Chaplain to George III, Henry Digby was born into a world of privilege, but not, as we shall see, to a life of ease.

Another uncle was one of Dorset's most famous Admirals, Sir Robert Digby, who with the prize money that he had won had purchased the Minterne Magna estate with its manor house. It was perfectly logical for Sir Robert's nephew to enter the Navy with such connections, and so, at the age of thirteen, he entered the service in 1783.

He was promoted to Lieutenant in 1790, and in 1795, when a Lieutenant on the *Pallas*, he helped save many of the crew of a ship that had accidentally caught fire. This was no easy task as all the guns were loaded and going off whenever they became engulfed by the flames, wounding and killing in every direction.

In the same year Digby was promoted to Commander, setting sail on the expedition to Quiberon Bay on the fire ship *Incendiary*. He then took command of the frigate *Aurora*, proving his worth to the British squadron attacking French and Spanish ships off the coast of Spain. He was promoted to Captain in 1796, and in 1798 he commanded the *Leviathan*, playing a prominent part in the capture of Minorca.

In 1799 he was appointed to the frigate *Alcmene*. Cruising between the coast of Portugal and the Azores, he chased and captured a Spanish frigate, a French corvette, a French privateer (the twenty-eight gun *La Courageuse*), and seven others, as well as destroying forty-eight sail of merchantmen. Throughout this command he showed skill at seamanship, as well as fearlessness, perhaps inherited from his uncle Sir Robert.

In the Bay of Biscay in October 1799, Digby assisted in one of the most audacious captures in naval history, that of the two Spanish treasure ships, the thirty-six gun *Thetis*, and the *Santa Brigida*, carrying forty guns, valuable merchandise and three million dollars in bullion.

It took fifty military wagons to convey the booty from Plymouth Dock, and by his own admission, Digby's share of prize money amounted to £57,000, a veritable fortune in today's money, in the region of three million pounds.

At Trafalgar, Digby's command, *Africa*, was, at sixty-four guns, the smallest vessel in the fleet, but he took a leading role in the battle, engaging the *Santissima Trinidada* in close combat. The huge, 140 gun Spanish four-decker was the biggest in the enemy fleet, and Digby's ship must have been dwarfed beside it. Fortunately for Digby, the enemy vessel was already seriously disabled, having been under fire from *Neptune*, *Leviathan* and *Conqueror*.

An amusing sidelight on the etiquette of warfare is that Digby, believing the *Santissima Trinidada* to be ready to surrender, sent a small boarding party under a Lieutenant on to the enemy vessel, only to be told by the Spaniards that they had no intention of doing any such thing. The boarding party were courteously but firmly ushered off and allowed to return to the *Africa* – meanwhile the battle raged on around them!

For his part in the battle Digby received the King's Trafalgar Gold Medal, the thanks of both Houses of Parliament and a sword of honour from the Lloyds Patriotic Fund. He returned home, married Lady Jane Elizabeth Coke, daughter of the first Earl of Leicester, and, on the death of his uncle, inherited the Minterne Magna estate in 1815, the same year that he was created a Companion of the Order of the Bath.

He was promoted to Rear-Admiral in 1819, to Vice-Admiral in 1830, and Admiral of the Blue in 1841. His final appointment was at Sheerness as Commander-in-Chief of the Nore from 1840-41.

Admiral Sir Henry Digby died at Minterne in 1842, aged 73, and was buried in the parish church of St Andrew, where a large brass on the south wall of the nave commemorates him, one of a trio of Dorset's heroic Captains at Trafalgar.

This is perhaps the place to pay tribute to Dorset's contribution to the Battle of Trafalgar as a whole. Eighteen Dorset men fought on *Victory*; the crew of Bullen's *Britannia* included ten local men; on

Digby's *Africa* there were three. Altogether, more than 180 Dorset men were aboard Nelson's fleet of thirty-three ships, serving in almost every capacity imaginable: there were Marines, Able Seamen, Gunners, Mates, Midshipmen, Ordinary Seamen and Boys – and many others, including pressed men and volunteers. They all had their part to play in Britain's greatest sea battle.

Sergeant William Lawrence (1791-1869), hero of Waterloo

A headstone in the churchyard of St Nicholas, Studland, tells the extraordinary story of William Lawrence, who ran away to the wars aged 14. As one of seven children of a Briantspuddle farm labourer, he experienced hardship from the day he was born. As a youngster he was paid 2d a day for frightening birds off the corn, and later he earned 6d a day working as a ploughboy.

His father wanted a better life for his fourteen-year old son, and, with a loan from a friend, purchased for him a seven-year apprenticeship with a Studland builder. Lawrence's new master had an evil temper, cutting short the boy's rations, criticising his work and even horsewhipping him when he answered back. This was more than enough for the strong-willed young man, who determined to run away, along with another apprentice who was being similarly treated. The two set off for Poole, where Lawrence hoped he would get work on board the Newfoundland packets, but the boys were caught, and Lawrence was sent back to Studland on the Swanage market boat.

On the way to Swanage word reached him that his master intended to get him sent to prison for reneging on the terms of his apprenticeship, so he escaped again, this time enlisting in the 40th Regiment of Foot. This was the start of a long period of service, lasting from 1805 to 1821, during which time he fought in the bloodiest and most celebrated battles of the Peninsular and Napoleonic Wars.

Lawrence cut a fine military figure. He was over six feet tall, and towered over the rest of his company. He was also a natural leader, and fearless, and was soon promoted to Corporal, and then to Sergeant.

In the heat of battle Lawrence had a number of close escapes, the luckiest perhaps being at the Battle of Badajoz in 1812. The injuries he received there were enough to send him to hospital for several months, but Lawrence always claimed that had his canteen not deflected the musket shot his injuries would certainly have been fatal.

Lawrence was well known for his sense of humour. He tamed a cockerel, naming it Tom, and carried the bird everywhere with him in his knapsack. At mealtimes Tom would flap his way round the other soldiers begging for titbits, always finding his way back to the right knapsack in time to accompany his master when the march resumed.

In his memoirs Lawrence admitted that when ordered to take the Colours at the Battle of Waterloo, he was not overjoyed at the prospect. Fourteen Colour Sergeants had already been killed or wounded on the battlefield, yet he earned personal praise from Wellington. Seeing Lawrence lead a successful skirmish against the French, Wellington approached him, asked his name and said in ringing tones: 'I shall think of you another day.'

After Waterloo, Lawrence was posted to Paris as part of the army of occupation. Outside his barrack gate there was a market, one of whose stalls was owned by a gardener from St Germain-en-Laye called Clairet. The stall was run by his daughter, Clotilde, who caught the eye of the 24-year-old redcoat. A blossoming romance followed, and Lawrence sought his colonel's permission to wed. Permission was granted, in spite of his colonel's surprise that one of his soldiers wanted to marry a Frenchwoman.

Clotilde dutifully stayed by her husband's side. In 1817, when garrisoned in Glasgow, Lawrence received news that his father was seriously ill. Given six weeks' leave of absence, the couple journeyed to Studland, where they were given a rapturous welcome. His elderly parents had never expected to see him alive again, and, of course, a French wife in tow caused quite a commotion. People came from far and wide to see the foreigner, because although French prisoners of war had been a common sight in the south of England for many years, few people had ever set eyes on a French *woman*.

When the Napoleonic Wars ended, the army reduced its numbers. In 1821 Lawrence was given an honourable discharge after 17 years and 7 months of service to his country. Because he still carried a slug shot in his knee from Badajoz, he was awarded a pension for life of 9d a day. He and Clotilde settled down in Studland as the popular landlord and landlady of the aptly-named Wellington Inn. Much later, when in his seventies, the illiterate Lawrence dictated his memoirs to a friend. The memoirs have survived and are an extraordinary first-hand account of the perilous life of a redcoat.

First and Second World Wars

Violet Cross(1891-1989), heroine of two World Wars

In 1916, two years after the outbreak of the First World War, Violet Norah Cross was twenty-four years old when she was appointed Matron in a field hospital in France, where she served with unstinting devotion to her patients.

At that time the full fury of the attacks on Verdun was filling hospitals to overflowing, and Violet Cross was hugely impressed by the quiet courage and patience of those she nursed. Soldiers lay on stretchers for three days and nights, waiting for admission to the operating theatres, whilst those who had had limbs amputated in the morning offered to go on stretchers on the floor the same evening to give up their beds to newcomers. For her outstanding work at Verdun, she was awarded the Croix de Guerre, a rare distinction for a British woman.

Between the wars, Violet Cross lived quietly in Hazelbury Bryan Manor House, which had been bought for his retirement by her father, the Reverend James Cross, Vicar of Sturminster Marshall for fifty-four years. Sadly, her father died only six months after his retirement, but she continued to live in the Manor House for more than half a century, giving her parish church of St Mary and St James every possible support, including the restoration, in 1938, of the chancel in her father's memory. She was also responsible for the construction of the lychgate at the church entrance, which won a Civic Trust award; for the restoration of several houses in the village (including almshouses), and for the conversion of some into a church room.

At the outbreak of the Second World War, the French surgeon, Dr Picot, under whom she had served in the Great War, cabled her, asking her to return to his side once more. She leapt at the chance, crossing to France in September 1939, arriving almost as soon as the British Expeditionary Force. She found that the hospital in Rouen had little more than the bare beds in it, so she returned to England for an intensive ten days' begging. She ended up with so many bales of bedding, clothing and equipment that she had to commandeer a French Army lorry to convey them from the docks to the train.

The 1940 German offensive brought turmoil. Refugees poured

through the streets – 'a pitiable and unforgettable sight', as she described it in *Wartime Escape*, her own account of her adventures.

Soon the medical team had to flee, boarding one of the last trains before the bridges were blown, arriving ten hours later at a château in Cabourg, just outside Caen. The senior medical officer took command, installing the nursing staff in the château and his men in the adjoining farm buildings. The next day he had the unenviable task of seeking out the German Kommandant and surrendering to him.

Violet was determined to escape. If it was found out that she was British she would certainly be sent to a concentration camp. The Germans ordered the team to St-Lô to take care of the 15,000 prisoners of war herded into barracks and buildings in the town.

The need to escape became ever more pressing. Her only hope was to get to Paris, where she had French friends who could assist her. Released from military service by the French, she and a fellow nurse, who had relatives in Paris, presented their demobilisation papers at the German headquarters. The Germans demanded to see their identity cards, which in Violet's case disclosed her British parentage on the inside pages. The friend presented hers first and it was minutely scrutinised. Then it was Violet's turn and, with despair in her heart, she handed over her card. Her name was copied down from the front, when, just at that moment, a German officer walked in and engaged the inspecting officer in urgent conversation. Her card was laid down, and a second later her hand slipped out from underneath her nursing cloak, retrieving the card. By the time the conversation came to an end the officer was so keen to make up for lost time, that he glanced down at his paperwork, saw that he had copied down two names and duly authorised two passes for the girls to 'go home' to Paris.

Once in Paris, another difficulty had to be surmounted, that of gaining the necessary permission at the Préfecture for travel to the Spanish frontier, which in turn had to be endorsed by the German authorities.

In the morning a sympathetic official at the Préfecture said: 'Come back at five, Mademoiselle, and I will see if I can get the preliminary visa, though I am not very hopeful.' Violet returned as requested, and after another long wait, was handed by the same official (with a smile), papers authorising her to leave Paris and travel to La Hendaye on the Spanish frontier.

Even so, crossing the frontier required German permission. Frightened out of her wits at their headquarters when confronted by a roomful of German officers, one of whom spoke guttural but fluent French, she sank into a chair, closed her eyes and prayed. Taking her to be weak and in distress, the German officers conferred, and stamped her papers, giving her full permission to cross the border.

From there Violet made her way to Lisbon, where she found a flying-boat shortly taking off for Britain with room for another passenger. The touch-down site could not have been more convenient, for she landed in Poole Harbour, and from there walked the last twenty-five miles or so back home to Hazelbury Bryan.

Shortly afterwards she enlisted as a private in the ATS, though she rose quickly to the rank of Junior Commander. After the invasion of Normandy she returned to the Continent, this time to help reunite children with their parents in Belgium and Holland.

After the war Violet Cross was given the freedom of the city of Caen. As a Dorset magistrate, she played a full part in local government, serving on parish, district and county councils (she was created an alderman of the County Council some eleven years before she retired in 1977).

Her conservation work included saving Bloxworth House and the Dower House at Kingston Maurward, and her enormous drive and enthusiasm contributed significantly to the protection of the county's heritage. In her own village she was a churchwarden for twenty-five years, and she was also president of the women's section of the Hazelbury Bryan Royal British Legion.

Miss Violet Cross died in 1989 and is buried in the place of her birth at Sturminster Marshall, though a plaque to her memory has been erected in the Stoke Wake chapel in Hazelbury Bryan church, bearing the inscription: 'I have fought a good fight. I have finished my course. I have kept the faith.'

Second World War

Wing-Commander Bill Loud (born 1920), Royal Air Force pilot

In 1942 Sergeant-Pilot Bill Loud was the pilot of a Spitfire which five German Messerschmitt fighters failed to bring down over France, when, to quote a record of the time, 'with bullet-torn rudder, he fought back, forcing one to turn away badly damaged. Battling to keep his own plane airborne, he outmanoeuvred the other four and flew safely home.'

Born in Bridport in August 1920, William Walter John Loud was educated at Poole Grammar School, later working as a butcher in his father's business, Messrs Soul & Son of Poole and Parkstone.

Volunteering for the RAF before his age group was called up, Loud, as he describes it, did 'two months square-bashing in Blackpool', before doing a month's training on Tiger Moths at North Luffenham in Rutland. On completion of his training he was promoted to Sergeant, achieving one of his proudest moments when, early in 1942, he joined the legendary flying ace Paddy Finucane's 602 Squadron at Kenley aerodrome near Redhill.

In July 1943 he was awarded the DFC, and promoted to Flight-Lieutenant soon afterwards. His official citation reads: 'Pilot Officer Loud has completed a large number of operational sorties, including shipping reconnaissances. He has destroyed at least one enemy aircraft and damaged others. This officer has always displayed an exceptional keenness to participate in operational flying and his courage and skill have been an example and inspiration to the other members of his squadron.'

Within a week of the D-Day landings in June 1944, Loud was flying sorties from a hastily prepared aerodrome south of Bayeux, which consisted of two fields knocked into one and a landing strip made of wire-netting to stop the ground from cutting up. The pilots and ground crew were housed in two-man tents, and Loud remembers that one night the enemy shelled the aerodrome from only two miles away. Most of the tents were destroyed and there were a number of casualties. Loud spent that particular night in an army tank in the next field, which he believes saved his life. The next day was spent, as Loud puts it, 'digging holes', but the airfield was not shelled again, the

German artillery post having been swiftly put out of action at dawn.

He was subsequently promoted to Flight-Commander, and in August 1944 commenced a second tour in command of 19 Squadron on Mustangs, being promoted in October 1944 to lead 122 Wing. By this time some of the sorties were over Belgium, and Loud vividly remembers blowing up a train carrying ammunition. Another task at this time was to dive-bomb the German invasion barges which were moored on the River Seine.

During the period 1 May 1942 to 15 August 1944, Loud's tally of enemy aircraft amounted to three (and one shared) 'destroyed', two 'probables' and two 'damaged', all over France. The rest of Loud's war was spent on escort of long-range bombing sorties. In December 1944 he received a Bar to his DFC, and in April 1945 he was awarded the DSO.

Loud and his group of 'veteran' pilots lasted the course, because they learned to combine prowess with experience, putting their first impulsive, even reckless, sorties behind them. As a Wing-Commander in the latter part of the war, Loud is on record as saying: 'The most dangerous period of a pilot's career is the first 20 sorties. If he survives that, then he stands a good chance of doing 300.'

Being himself a living example of his own words, Loud went back to work as a butcher in Poole. In 1948 he entered hotel management, which occupied the rest of his working life. He retired to the place of his birth, Bridport, where he now lives in West Bay.

Lieutenant-Commander Kenneth Pattisson (1916-2002), Fleet Air Arm Swordfish pilot

As a Swordfish pilot in 810 Squadron, Kenneth Pattisson was one of the Fleet Air Arm flyers who carried out the attack which crippled the *Bismarck* in May 1941, and, by all accounts, it was probably his torpedo that did the damage.

The attack, by thirteen Swordfish launched from *Ark Royal*, scored two hits on the heavily-armoured German battleship, one of which, by an extraordinarily lucky chance, decisively damaged her steering gear, so that all she could do was circle out of control, allowing the Home Fleet to close in and finish her off.

In bad visibility Pattisson had become separated from his flight commander, but as he dived below the cloud base at 800 feet, having already been hit by flak, he spotted the German battleship and launched his attack at a range of 900 yards. To aim effectively Pattisson used a row of lights on the Swordfish's wing as a guide to how far ahead to aim, each light representing five knots of target speed, as well as having to make allowance for *Bismarck* turning. At the absurdly low speed of 90 knots, Pattisson's Swordfish was a sitting duck, and the *Bismarck* was blazing away at him with everything she had. Miraculously, Pattisson was not hit, and he had the satisfaction of seeing his torpedo down and running towards the German battleship.

At dawn the next day, Pattisson and his crew were re-launched from the *Ark Royal* to finish the *Bismarck* off, but when they readied themselves to dive for the attack, it was plain that they had already done enough. The *Bismarck* was listing heavily to port and on fire, being pounded by the battleships *King George V* and *Rodney*.

Incredible as it seems, a small force of biplane aircraft, looking more at home in the Great War than in World War Two, had risen to the occasion and put a modern capital ship out of action.

The coup de grâce that sent the *Bismarck* beneath the waves was delivered at 10.36 in the morning on Monday 26 May 1941 by means of torpedoes fired from the cruiser *Dorsetshire*, completing the work begun by the Fleet Air Arm. For his part in this momentous conclusion Pattisson was awarded the DSC.

His squadron, No 810, was disbanded four months after the *Bismarck* action, but was re-formed, operating Fireflies from the aircraft carrier *Theseus*, during the Korean War. In 1954 Pattisson converted to jets at RNAS Culdrose, before retiring from the Navy in 1958, some eight years after he had come to live in Dorset.

His flying career had spanned twenty years in which he had survived more than 400 deck landings. His passion for sailing was passed down to his son, Rodney, triple Olympic yachting medallist *(see page 71)*. Kenneth Pattisson's little tan-sailed lugger was a familiar sight among the creeks and islands of Poole Harbour until the year before he died in 2002, aged 85.

Alasdair Ferguson, MBE, DSC and Bar (1919-2004),
Landing Craft Commander at Dieppe and on D-Day

Sub-Lieutenant Alasdair Forbes Ferguson, RNVR was second-in-command of the 10th Landing Craft Assault (LCA) Flotilla that took part in the debacle of the Dieppe raid on 19 August 1942.

The politically motivated operation was doomed to failure from the outset, being too large to qualify as a raid and too small to succeed as an invasion. Furthermore, it was imprecise in its objectives and had an unworkably complicated operational plan.

None of that detracted from the bravery of those who fought against the odds, as, by a most unfortunate chance, a German coastal convoy became entangled with the assault force, leading to disorganisation of the landing craft and alerting the garrison.

As if that misfortune was not enough, the Royal Regiment of Canada found themselves pinned against a sea wall on Puys beach in full view of the enemy. No ship could get close to rescue them and the survivors had to surrender. Of the 556 men of the Royal Regiment of Canada who had sailed for Dieppe, more than 200 died and 264 were captured.

Having disembarked his unfortunate Canadians, Ferguson managed to get back to his parent ship, and then, following the plan to withdraw after several hours, was sent back to the main beach with four landing craft to try to recover survivors. Two were sunk and Ferguson's landing craft, severely overloaded, pulled away under heavy fire and was itself hit. He transferred his passengers to another, for which he was mentioned in despatches.

After this episode, Ferguson continued to serve on landing craft, alternating between Combined Operations training units and assault landing operations.

In November 1942 he commanded the 60th LCA Flotilla for Operation Torch, the Allied landings in North Africa, carrying US troops ashore. His command continued in the invasion of Sicily in July 1943 and the bloody assault at Salerno in September.

Ferguson was awarded the DSC in 1944, and was described by a contemporary as 'a natural born leader, with great aplomb and quiet courage – in everything he did he required the highest standard of organisation while caring for all his sailors.'

In the D-Day invasion, Ferguson carried the 1st Battalion The Hampshire Regiment to Gold Beach and the strongpoint of Le Hamel, and was later awarded a Bar to his DSC for his courage and leadership.

After the war he began a long and distinguished association with Poole, becoming managing director of Hamworthy Engineering, overseeing a period of rapid growth. In 1958, with his brother Nick, he bought Bourne Steel, which at that time had only fifteen employees, turning it into a 160-strong company with a major foothold in the Middle East, one of the top five in its field in the UK.

He was chairman of the Sub-Commissioners of Trinity House, Poole, managing pilotage in the area for 27 years. He founded the Poole Maritime Trust, which supported the exploration of a sixteenth century wreck in Studland Bay, and he played a key rôle in the preservation of the Waterfront Museum. To embellish the waterfront, he bought and installed a sculpture by Sir Anthony Caro. Like so many who come to live in Poole, he was a keen sailor, often sailing his yacht *Swan of Arden* to France.

Alasdair Ferguson died on 26 December 2004, aged 85, having lived through some of the most hair-raising events of the Second World War. Of those courageous landing craft personnel, Admiral Vian wrote simply: 'Their spirit and seamanship rose to meet the greatness of the hour.'

Reg Hyde (1922-1979), 'McIndoe's Army' Guinea Pig

Reg Hyde was a member of that elite band of airmen, the 'Guinea Pig Club', a group of patients treated by Archibald (later Sir Archibald) McIndoe and his special burns team at East Grinstead.

Born at 133 Wimborne Road, Poole, Hyde went to Poole Grammar School, and then got a job working at the Municipal Buildings. In 1940, he joined the RAF as a Flight Sergeant Observer.

He flew in a great number of sorties across enemy territory, but the accident that led to his injuries occurred while he was training pilots to fly Wellington bombers in the skies above Buckinghamshire.

Following a training flight, the Wellington's port engine failed just before touchdown. Unfortunately, there was another aircraft on the runway. The moment Hyde spotted it, he knew that he would not have enough power to clear it and make a second attempt at landing. He chose the only alternative, steering the Wellington past the obstruction and crash landing in the scrub beside the runway.

The Wellington smashed into two trees, and Hyde, wearing neither gloves nor helmet, found himself in an inferno. Finding superhuman strength, which he never quite understood, he forced the astrodome cover open and jumped on to one of the torn-off wings. He was up to his knees in flames and knew that he must get away before the plane exploded. He scrambled off the wing, pushed his way through a barbed wire fence and fell into a ditch. At that moment the plane went up, but the full force of the blast missed him.

Picked up by a rescue team who were astonished to find him still alive, Hyde was driven to hospital where he was at first unable to open his mouth and had to be fed through a tube. It was not until he was transferred to East Grinstead that his mouth was sufficiently restored for him to be able to eat.

Month after month went by, and operation after operation; by the time Hyde was fit to leave he had undergone about a hundred operations, not all successful, as the study of tissue matching was in its infancy and many of the grafts did not take. But Hyde's (and others') failed operations allowed Archibald McIndoe and his team to build up unprecedented knowledge in the field, resulting in the East Grinstead centre's recognition as the world leader in plastic surgery.

Part of McIndoe's success was not just the physical rehabilitation that he gave to his patients, but social rehabilitation as well. They would go off down to the pub and socialise with the locals, who were used to their disfigurements and treated them with courtesy and respect.

Just as remarkable as Hyde's recovery was his subsequent career. His appalling burns meant that he had undergone one of the longest programmes of medical treatment of any Club member. But in the recovery ward Hyde had met and, a year later, married one of the staff nurses, Jean Fuggle.

They had three children and Hyde landed a job as a planner, rising to Executive Engineer responsible for the Crawley New Town project. At the height of his career he was a man with an exceptional memory, who could retain details in his mind which most other people would have to search for in a filing cabinet. Passionate about planning, he went to America, where he studied bridges, roads and out-of-town developments, constantly searching for ideas to bring back to Crawley.

The town is a monument to his diligence and inspiration.

When Hyde died, on 3 March 1979, one of the biggest ever gatherings of Guinea Pigs assembled in St Margaret's Church, Ifield, near Crawley, to pay him tribute. In life he had been the man responsible for planning, building and maintaining the maze of neat roads which make up Crawley New Town. It would not have been lost on his friends and colleagues that they were driving along these same roads to reach the church.

George Millar (1910-2005),
SOE officer who organised Maquis saboteurs

Although Scottish born, George Reid Millar made Dorset his home after the war, spending nearly fifty years farming at Sydling Court, Sydling St Nicholas.

Originally planning to become an architect, Millar then turned his hand to journalism, and, like so many, was overtaken by events when war broke out. He trained as an officer with the Special Operations Executive, formed on Winston Churchill's order to 'set Europe ablaze' after the fall of France in 1940.

In the early stages of the war he was wounded and captured at Gazala in June 1942 and shipped to Italy, where he was put into a POW camp near Taranto. His skill at masterminding clandestine operations quickly became apparent, when he organised the buying of black-market food from outside the camp. He played female parts in prisoners' theatricals, and, as one inmate was to relate, 'while others were forming escape committees and drawing up rotas for tunnelling parties, Millar was planning to climb over the wire dressed as a nun.'

His opportunity to escape came when the prisoners were being sent to Germany by rail after the collapse of Italy in 1943. Jumping from the train at night near Munich, he made an extraordinary journey via Strasbourg to Paris, where Mara Scherbatov, a White Russian princess, gave him money to complete his journey across France and then through Spain to Gibraltar and safety.

Available again for active service, Millar was given parachute training and was dropped into France on 1 June 1944, to work with the Maquis in delaying German troop movements from the South of France to the Normandy battlefields in the days immediately preceding the D-Day landings.

He established the SOE 'Chancellor' network in the region and embarked on a series of sabotage operations in conjunction with the Maquis, whose confidence he had quickly won. He and his saboteurs caused such disruption to the Besançon marshalling yards that Millar advised SOE's headquarters in Baker Street against an RAF bombing attack on the yards – this had the welcome side-effect of preserving the city's seventeenth century architecture from almost certain destruction.

His courage in the Western desert and subsequent escape from the train carrying him to prison camp in Germany had already been recognised by the award of the Military Cross. His time with the Maquis resulted in Millar being awarded the DSO, the Légion d'Honneur and the Croix de Guerre.

After the war he married Isabel Paske-Smith and sailed the Mediterranean for a while, but he yearned for peace and quiet in the country. Coming from farming stock, he turned to sheep and cattle rearing on the thousand acres adjoining Sydling Court, before finally moving to Uploders and living out his days in his adopted county of Dorset.

Dodo Selby Bennett (1920-1991),
nurse with the wartime Maquis, politician and journalist

If ever the phrase 'lived life to the full' was applicable, then Dodo Selby Bennett (née Lees) would be top of the list of contenders. Her life story makes breathless reading, and it is difficult to capture in a few words the remarkable things that she achieved in her seventy-one years.

Coming from a marriage of two landowning Dorset families, Lees and Weld, and christened Dolores (a name she hated), she admitted that she had been born 'with a silver spoon in her mouth', but her warm-hearted nature won her many friends, who were able to open doors when needed.

Stunningly attractive, Dodo only had to walk into a room to be noticed, and through her 'deb' days she fell in and out of love like a yo-yo, but underneath her extrovert exterior there was a steely determination that was to be the making of her, as well as getting her into countless scrapes.

As a young journalist, she saved up enough to go to Germany to visit Irmchen, a girl she had befriended on the Isle of Wight. Arriving in Breslau, she found herself in a sinister atmosphere of anti-Semitic

36

fervour. Jews – friends of her German friends – were being arrested and just disappearing. Dodo's British passport came to the rescue for Irmchen's brother's Jewish girlfriend and her 11-year-old daughter, who used it to escape across the Austrian border, after which the passport was returned to Dodo by a Jewish underground organisation.

Returning to England in May 1939, she knew that this chilling experience had hardened her views about the Nazis, and when war broke out four months later, she was determined to play her part in defeating them. She worked first as a Voluntary Aid Detachment (VAD) nurse, and then, taking advantage of her family connection with the Chief of the Imperial General Staff, Lord Alanbrooke, she persuaded Ernest Bevin, the Minister of Labour, to allow her to join the French Red Cross as an ambulance driver.

She served with the 6th Colonial Infantry Regiment in the French First Army, and saw service during the Rhine and Danube campaigns and in the battle of the Colmar Gap, subsequently taking part in the liberation of Dachau concentration camp and tending the inmates.

In the winter of 1944-45, she was approached by Resistance fighters from the Vosges mountains and asked to tend their wounded, which involved crossing the German lines, disguised as a civilian, and living with the Maquis in a cave. She was awarded the Croix de Guerre and Bar for rescuing wounded men under fire and in minefields.

After the war, by now a well-known figure in the French Army, she was, despite her British nationality, made an officer and appointed personal staff officer to Marshal Leclerc, the French commander of armoured units on D-Day, who had accepted the surrender of German-occupied Paris in August 1944. When Leclerc died in an air crash in November 1947, Dodo Lees was seconded to the French Foreign Office and sent to make a series of lecture tours in America, informing audiences in the United States of French feelings about the Marshall Plan.

Many years earlier, aged fourteen, Dodo had been deeply affected by a visit to Brandon Colliery, where she had been taken down the mine which was about to close. She never forgot the dank and airless passages through which she crawled, nor the pickaxe-wielding miners, covered in coal dust, poorly paid and about to lose their livelihood. At that moment, she vowed to join the Labour Party when she grew up. Her resolve never weakened. She fought Brendan Bracken in

Bournemouth East in 1949, and nearly unseated her cousin, Sir Fitzroy Maclean, another wartime hero, in Lancaster in 1951. In 1953, a week before she married naval officer 'Chipps' Selby Bennett, she was offered a safe Labour seat, but she felt that a political career was incompatible with following her husband around the world, although later on, in 1962, she played a key role in ensuring a Labour victory for Guy Barnett in South Dorset, hitherto staunchly Conservative.

In 1955 Selby Bennett was posted to Malta, where Dodo's influential cousins, the Stricklands, lived. An introduction to Prime Minister Dom Mintoff was arranged and in a short time Dodo was virtually co-opted into his government. He put her in charge of tourism, and thus she contributed to the extraordinary change in Malta's standard of living. She remained on friendly terms with Mintoff and his English wife, playing a behind the scenes role in curbing his anti-British excesses when he was re-elected prime minister in 1971.

In 1966 Commander Selby Bennett was appointed defence attaché in Venezuela, Colombia, Panama and the Dominican Republic, and for the next three years Dodo travelled extensively in Latin America.

Always fiercely independent, she took her own line, even canvassing against her own husband when he stood for the Dorset County Council as a Conservative.

Dodo Selby Bennett was one of life's extraordinary characters. She spoke fluent French and German, and she mastered many other foreign languages. She was completely unafraid of danger and she was one of those rare people who touched the life of anyone she met. They numbered in their thousands.

Michael Lees (1921-1992), wartime hero

Michael Lees was Dodo's brother, and his wartime exploits were as remarkable as his sister's. To help to understand their character it is a good idea to look at the stock from which they came.

Their grandfather was Sir John Elliot Lees, of South Lytchett House. Member of Parliament for Oldham, and then Birkenhead, he was a director of the *People* newspaper and Master of the South Dorset Hunt. He also commanded the 26th Dorsetshire Company of the Imperial Yeomanry in the Boer War, returning from South Africa with the DSO.

Sir John's eldest son, Sir Thomas Evans Keith Lees, was killed at Gallipoli, his second son, Captain Sir John Victor Elliot Lees, was severely wounded in Flanders, and his third son, Captain Bernard Percy Turnbull Lees, father of Dodo and Michael, served in the Great War with the Dorset Yeomanry.

It was into this military world that Michael and Dodo Lees were born soon after the end of the Great War. By 1939 Michael Lees was an eighteen year old raring for action, and his chance came in June 1943 when he was parachuted into Yugoslavia as leader of a Special Operations Executive (SOE) mission to liaise with Chetnik guerrillas.

They fell into the hands of a Bulgarian unit and many of Lees' wounded men were butchered where they lay. He managed to regroup and persuaded General Mihailovic to blow up two strategic sections of railway and six German trains.

Then the Allies changed allegiance, from Mihailovic's Serbs to Tito's partisans, and Lees spent the next forty-five years trying to uncover what had led to the British volte-face, which had imposed communism on Yugoslavia instead of supporting its monarchy. Mihailovic and his men remained loyal to their King and the Allies, but they were arrested by Tito and executed as traitors. Lees never forgot his former friends and he left no stone unturned in trying expose the duplicity involved. In the end he put it down to Winston Churchill being hoodwinked by one-sided intelligence.

Lees was withdrawn to Italy, where he met and married Gwen Johnson, who was a FANY nurse (First Aid Nursing Yeomanry). He was then parachuted back into action to escort two delegates from the Piedmontese Liberation Committee over the Maritime Alps, en route destroying a German artillery post in order to reach the safety of the American lines.

His next mission, with SAS Major Roy Farren, was to attack a German HQ in an Albanian villa, in the course of which Lees was shot. Collapsing down a stairwell with four bullets in him, he escaped by being hidden under manure in an ox-cart, which carried him to a mountain terrace. There he took off in a spotter-plane, which flew him to Naples to receive the urgent attention he needed at a hospital there.

Making a remarkable recovery, he returned to England where he mounted his campaign to bring to light the story of General Mihailovic's downfall. He published an account in 1990 and was fêted in Yugoslavia where he predicted that the Serbs would again lose out, this time to the Croats.

After his death in 1992 the *Times* obituary eloquently summed up Michael Lees' character: 'Lees spent the day he died at his desk intent on his crusade. He had brought to it the great force of his personality, the single-mindedness and the courage which had characterised his life. It is not given to many men to die happy in fighting a cause first embraced in youth.'

The heroic airmen of Tarrant Rushton,
Second World War aerodrome

Tarrant Rushton played such a key role in the Second World War that I have used it as an umbrella heading to mention those whose heroism began here, even though the men involved were not necessarily of Dorset stock.

It was from this airfield that paratroopers flew for practice drops over Cranborne Chase, first by day and then by night; and it was the airfield's proximity to the Normandy coast that led to its central role in the invasion. The two aerodromes closest to the selected drop-zones were Tarrant Rushton and nearby RAF Hurn, and it was the men who took off from Tarrant Rushton who had the distinction of being amongst the first Allied troops to land in France on D-Day.

In the early hours of 6th June 1944 two Horsa gliders and a fleet of 30 Hamilcars were towed into the air by Halifax tug-planes, and released silently over France for their perilous mission. Emerging from one of the Horsa gliders, Major John Howard and his five companions (D Company, 2nd Battalion, Oxfordshire and Buckinghamshire Light Infantry) were the first to step onto French soil. They immediately made for and seized the Orne Canal bridge, which would be a vital crossing for ground forces when they arrived. The bridge is now better known as Pegasus Bridge (from the men's flying-horse emblem) and is one of the most visited sites connected with the D-Day Landings.

Tarrant Rushton had a part to play at two more key moments in 1944. In September, the same Halifaxes towed 96 gliders containing men of the British 1st Airborne Division to Arnhem and the disaster of 'A Bridge Too Far'. Amongst the many heroes in this engagement were the 250 men of the 4th Battalion of the Dorsetshire Regiment, who maintained a ceaseless shuttle of assault boats across the Lower Rhine, bringing back battle-weary paratroopers from the Arnhem bridgehead, until daylight gave German firepower the advantage of pinpoint accuracy, whereupon all further rescue attempts became impossible. The Dorsetshire Regiment won two Military Crosses (Captain Ronald Hall and Captain Dennis McDermott) and a Military Medal (Private Lionel Driver) for bravery in this action.

Three months later, in the wintriest December for years, the German Army began its final offensive in the Ardennes. Casualties streamed into Dorset via Tarrant Rushton. Up to 500 American wounded were flown in by C-47 Dakotas in a single night and taken to the 22nd General Hospital of the US Army at Blandford Camp.

Towards the end of the war sixty Halifax tug-planes with their Horsa and Hamilcar gliders left for RAF Woodbridge in Suffolk from where they transported the British 6th Airborne Division to be dropped behind the Rhine in Operation Varsity. Fifty-two of the Tarrant Rushton gliders landed successfully in daytime, and with this final airborne offensive Tarrant Rushton ceased to be a front-line airbase.

But its story did not end there, because Tarrant Rushton became the main base for Sir Alan Cobham's company, Flight Refuelling Limited (*see page 112*). When Soviet forces cut the rail and road links between West Germany and Berlin in July 1948, Sir Alan's bulk fuel tankers were requisitioned. Flying from Tarrant Rushton throughout the Berlin airlift, they transported a total of 26,000 tons of fuel over fourteen months in a determined effort to break the Berlin blockade.

In 1949, Flight Refuelling Limited set an international endurance record when Pat Hornidge kept a Meteor jet in the air for more than twelve hours. In 1982, air-to-air refuelling enabled a Vulcan bomber to fly from Ascension Island to Port Stanley airfield during the Falklands War.

The company, FR Group plc, is still based in Dorset, at nearby Wimborne, but by the early 1970s it no longer needed its Tarrant Rushton airfield. The runways were bulldozed and turned back into farmland, leaving a war memorial and single hanger, but almost no trace of a site unique in the history of aviation.

Betty Hockey (born 1916), wartime entertainer, and her tribute to the 'Forgotten Army', the men who fought in Burma

I owe this article entirely to Mrs Betty Hockey, who was born and bred in Bournemouth, and who lives there still. She is a hero herself, but she drew my attention to a group of soldiers whose story is untold until now.

In 1940 Betty was working in the Army Record Office, when she decided it was 'time for a change'. She applied for a transfer to a job collecting tyres for re-treading, which involved travelling all around the Southern Command area. Finding that this gave her unique contact with army units, she applied for permission to start up a 'concert party' along the lines of ENSA.

Permission was granted and Betty placed an advertisement in the *Echo*, receiving a huge response. She interviewed and whittled down the hopefuls to a group of sixteen, who were required to attend local dancing school to learn their trade. They were put through their paces and they kitted themselves out in costumes obtained from 'granny's attic'.

From the start their performances were hugely popular, and when Betty recalls that their programme included the can-can, a fan dance and the 'Dance of the Seven Veils', it is easy to understand why the show went down so well with the troops.

The most moving part of her story continues in the letter that she first wrote to me – reproduced here in her own unforgettable words:

'During W.W.II I ran a Southern Command Concert Party for the Forces, clocking up well over 1,000 shows prior to D-Day. Many of these were wallowing in mud waiting to go to France. But nothing will erase the scene of the 'Forgotten Army' as we witnessed, hence this letter.

'On November 24th 1945 I received a telephone call requesting the Concert Party to go to 68th Transit Camp on Southampton Common that same evening. Thinking it to be just another troop show, off we went.

'In hindsight I feel that we should have been warned what to expect, but imagine our surprise when we were confronted with a sea of men, broken in health and spirit, far too ill and weak to sit watching a show. Most had missing teeth caused by being battered by rifles, some jabbering away incoherently and some near to passing out after the ordeal of travelling on the boats which had just brought them back from Burma.

'Under the circumstances, all we could do was to squat on the floor by their side and gently talk to them or listen to their tales of woe. They were brought in just lying on mattresses waiting to be sent to hospitals, homes or to the bosom of their families, those latter, if they were able.

'Apart from the doctors, nurses and carers I suppose we were the first British people they had seen in ages, and they were so happy to be back, at least those of sound mind. The rest were indeed in so much shock and pain there was little we could do for them but just to sit holding their hands, which is what they wanted to do most of all.

'Looking back I feel privileged indeed that *we* were called to these wonderfully brave men and I often wonder how many of them made it back to health *and give thanks to God* that we had the privilege to be there for them at that terrible time.

'Very few were in condition to even write their names in my book, but I do have just a few which may help you. We did five nights in a row for several weeks whilst these fine men and boys were being brought back to this country, but I will *never* forget that shock we received of the condition they were all in.

'All our great veterans have now had their share of glory and rightfully so. It surely now is the time to honour all these of the 'Forgotten Army'.'

Characteristically, Betty puts her desire to make certain that these brave men are remembered above her own deserving claim to recognition. But her initiative in founding the Southern Command Concert Party must surely rank as one of the most unusual of the war effort.

Known as the 'Nonstops Variety Troop Show', it was the only one of the shows that ran for two hours non-stop – a boon as far as the camp authorities were concerned, because in other shows with breaks, soldiers drifted to the bar and then did not return. The troupe had four different shows – a South Sea skit with hula-hula girls, a Parisian café with can-can, a Western, and a sketch with an oriental theme. Betty and her 'troupers' were hugely popular wherever they went, receiving help with transport, loading and unloading of scenery and props, and provision of dressing rooms in venues ranging from fully-equipped camp theatres to performing on the flatbed of an army truck, known as 'tailboard' shows.

During its eight years of existence (1940-48), the troupe performed at eighty or more Army camps, Air Force bases or Royal Navy ships, and when the American Forces joined the war, the 'Nonstops' visited a dozen or more US units based in the area.

In recognition of Betty's invaluable, morale-boosting contribution, the State of Maryland made her an honorary citizen, and when the tall ship *Pride of Baltimore* sailed to Britain and put in at Weymouth, the Governor of Maryland alerted her, so that she could be welcomed on board.

Since the war, Betty has revisited all camps, bases and units that are still operational, and each year she attends a veterans' reunion in a different US state. She has been given the 'freedom' of six Royal Navy ships, including the *Ark Royal*, the *Illustrious* and the *Invincible*, and she has an open pass to Blandford Camp.

She welcomes parties of veterans from the US and organises visits to former Army and Air Force bases, in one case laying on a US Army Jeep complete with authentic insignia, much to the astonishment of the visitors. Still not a day goes by without her going out and about, responding to the countless invitations that she receives, or fielding enquiries about her colourful past.

The remarkable Betty Hockey now lives in a former tennis pavilion in Southbourne, amongst her collection of dolls, her mountains of memorabilia, and her memories, which she is happy to share, giving vivid accounts of her extraordinary life, undimmed by the passing of time.

THREE

For those in Peril on the Sea

Since the foundation of the Royal National Lifeboat Institution in 1824, just over 2,400 medals – gold, silver and, since 1917, bronze – have been awarded for gallantry in saving life from shipwreck.

This chapter records, chronologically, the gallant deeds of all the Dorset men (and two lads) who were awarded medals, as well as the very first medal awarded by the Institution to Commander Fremantle in 1824 for his part in an incident which occurred off Christchurch.

The following is taken from *Lifeboat Gallantry, The Complete Record of Royal National Lifeboat Institution Gallantry Medals and how they were won, 1824-1996*, edited by Barry Cox, Honorary Librarian RNLI, to whom I am indebted for allowing me to reproduce his text (with minor adaptations).

Commander Charles Howe Fremantle, RN, Commander HM Coastguard, Lymington (Gold)

8 March 1824: The Swedish brig *Carl Jean*, Peter Wabrood, Master, bound from Alicante to Gefle, laden with wine, was seen to be in difficulties broadside on to the shore at Whitepit, near Christchurch.

The mainmast was overside and the vessel striking so heavily that it looked as if she would break up. Commander Fremantle managed to reach her by swimming through the surf with a line fastened to his body.

Although he had the ship's boats cut clear, heavy seas filled them, rendering them useless. When he proposed other rescue measures, the brig's crew refused to act on them. He returned to the shore only with the help of a shore line by which he was hauled in, exhausted and insensible. Eventually, after the ship broke up, her crew reached shore using the wreck of the mainmast.

In 1829, when in command of the frigate *HMS Challenger*,

Fremantle was specially selected to take possession of Western Australia, and the port of Fremantle is named after him. The district of Swanbourne in Western Australia is named after the village in Buckinghamshire where his family seat is situated.

He commanded the Channel Fleet and became Commander-in-Chief at Devonport in 1861, and afterwards was knighted.

Lieutenant William Parsons, HM Coastguard, Swanage (Silver)

7 April 1838: The French vessel *L'Aimable Mère*, in passage from Bordeaux to Dunkirk, was wrecked during stormy weather off St Aldhelm's Head. Lieutenant Parsons, with a crew of seven of his men, launched his galley from Swanage and saved the Master and six men, bringing them safely ashore.

Lieutenant George Davies, RN, Gunner Edward Leggett, Seaman Charles Stubbs, Revenue Cutter *Tartar* (all Silver)

11 March 1839: The French brig *Le Jean Marie* from Bordeaux was in danger of being wrecked near Swanage with her Master and seven men on board. Lieutenant Davies and his two men put off in a boat and brought the brig to port.

John Hansford, Portland (Silver)

30 November 1841: In a heavy south-west gale, the brig *Amyntas* was wrecked in West Bay on passage from Quebec to Exeter, laden with timber. She ground to a halt in heavy surf and her Master and three men were drowned in trying to reach the shore. Two others were saved by Mr Hansford, a brave Portlander, who rushed into the breakers and brought them ashore.

Joseph White and William Flann (both Silver)

30 December 1860: The Plymouth schooner *Norval* was wrecked on Chesil Beach in a gale. Messrs White and Flann, in company with five others, put off in a boat and rescued her crew of five. White had also assisted in saving 43 persons and Flann 57 from previous wrecks.

John Lose, Chief Officer, HM Coastguard, Swanage (Silver)

23 January 1875: The Exeter brigantine *Wild Wave*, bound for Poole with a cargo of coal, was wrecked off Peveril Point in a gale and heavy sea. *Wild Wave* was firmly jammed on the rocks, her main mast gone by the board. Twelve coastguards, with Mr Lose, put off in two four-oared gigs to the rescue, but were unable to reach the wreck.

At dawn five survivors were seen in the rigging; Mr Lose again put out and, as the gale abated, was able to bring off four men and a boy. Shortly afterwards, the wreck slipped from the rocks and sank below the sea. The young boy, an orphan, was adopted by a Poole painter who apprenticed him to his own trade.

As a direct result of this incident, the RNLI decided to place a lifeboat at Swanage.

Frank Perry and Frederick Carter (both Silver)

26 May 1890: In a strong easterly breeze and heavy surf, a boat capsized in Weymouth Bay and two men were thrown out. This was seen by two lads, Frank Perry, aged 16, and Frederick Carter, aged 11, who were in another boat in smooth water. They rowed into the broken water and saved one of the men.

Robert Charles Brown, Assistant Mechanic, Swanage Lifeboat (Bronze)

19 March 1934: When the yacht *Hally Lise* appeared to be in difficulties off Southbourne, the self-righting motor lifeboat *Thomas Markby* launched in a strong southerly gale and heavy seas. When she came up with the yacht at 1.30pm it was near Boscombe Pier and close to the shore. The waves were eight feet high and, as the lifeboat approached, the yacht struck and was thrown on its beam ends. One of the two men on board was thrown into the sea, and Mr Brown went overboard in oilskins, lifebelt and sea boots, seized him and held him until both were picked up. The other man was rescued from the shore by life saving apparatus.

Frederick James Palmer, Coxswain, Weymouth Lifeboat (Bronze)
6-7 June 1948: When 15 miles west of Portland Bill, a converted 110ft naval motor launch, now the twin screw motor yacht *Mite*, suffered failure of both wireless and engines. With a fresh wind increasing, two of her crew volunteered to make for the shore and seek help.

The Coastguard had seen the dinghy driving ashore and alerted the Weymouth lifeboat station. Five minutes after the dinghy landed, the Barnett class lifeboat *William and Clara Ryland* slipped her moorings and reached the yacht, now anchored, at 4.30pm.

The owner requested a tow and, reluctantly, Coxswain Palmer agreed. In seriously worsening conditions on a course wide of Portland Bill, the lifeboat towed the yacht for 12 miles. After the tow parted for the third time at 8.30pm, two miles off the Shambles, the yacht's three man crew was taken off. The yacht was washed ashore later near Lulworth Cove.

Frederick James Palmer, Coxswain (Silver) and
James McDermott, Mechanic (Bronze), Weymouth Lifeboat
2 April 1949: In heavy rain driven by a strong south-westerly wind and dense banks of fog over a rough sea, the old dockyard steam tug *HLS 161*, in passage from Plymouth to London, was reported in difficulties west of Portland Bill and drifting northwards.

The Weymouth lifeboat put to sea and, after searching in the fog, found the tug, her steering almost out of action, broadside on to the Chesil Beach 50 yards away. Losing no time, Coxswain Palmer took his lifeboat alongside, managed to get a tow on board, and pulled the tug off just in time to avoid certain death for the four men on board. It was then 8.20am. Two hours later they reached Weymouth.

Donald Shipwey Laker, Crew Member, Weymouth Lifeboat (Bronze)
29 May 1965: In the early afternoon, the yacht *Dehra* went aground to the north of the pier at Weymouth, in a moderate wind and a short, choppy sea with spray breaking over her. Successive efforts were made to help her by the Barnett class lifeboat *Frank Spiller Locke*, a small boat, and by rockets.

The Coxswain decided that to wait any longer would mean the yacht being driven up the beach on her beam ends. Mr Laker went overside and swam to her with a line, after stripping to his underclothes. With the tow secured and the yacht's owner and one of his crew injured, the lifeboat held the yacht's head to wind until she refloated with the tide and was taken into harbour.

Ronald James Hardy, Coxswain, Swanage Lifeboat (Bronze)

12 September 1970: After returning from a previous service, most of the crew of the Watson class lifeboat *R.L.P.* were still in the boathouse when they were asked to launch again. She slipped her moorings at 5pm.

A youth was trapped by the rising tide in a cave to the west of Blacker's Hole where the lifeboat arrived half an hour later to find a big swell breaking heavily at the foot of the cliff, its backwash creating a nasty, confused sea. The youth was standing on a ledge at the back of the cave, the floor was awash and covered with boulders. After the lifeboat had veered down as near as possible, he was brought out using the inflatable dinghy.

John Leslie Hodder, Crew Member, Lyme Regis Inshore Lifeboat (Bronze)

14 March 1971: While working on The Cobb at Lyme Regis, John Hodder heard cries for help; the inflatable lifeboat being out of action, he ran around the harbour to alert the skipper and owner of the motor fishing vessel *Barbarella*. The vessel put out at 7.40pm in a north-westerly wind and short choppy sea. The skipper's son and another boy had been out in their fishing dinghy hauling pots but had got into difficulties.

About 500 yards offshore, the skipper's son was seen in the water. John Hodder dived into the sea, followed immediately by the boy's father, who had to be rescued a short time later. Mr Hodder was then found supporting the boy and, cold and exhausted, they were landed without delay. Extensive searches by the vessel together with another fishing boat, the Exmouth lifeboat and a naval helicopter failed to find the other boy.

Alfred Thomas Pavey, Coxswain, Weymouth Lifeboat (Bronze)

4-5 February 1972: The gas tanker *Methane Princess* reported the yacht *Nomis* in distress off Portland Bill, with the skipper in need of medical attention. The Barnett class lifeboat *Frank Spiller Locke* left her moorings at 10pm with the Honorary Medical Adviser on board.

A south-south-east gale was blowing over a very rough sea, and the *Methane Princess* reported that she had had to abandon her tow. Reaching the casualty shortly after midnight, Coxswain Pavey took the lifeboat alongside allowing the bowman and Dr Parkinson to jump on board.

As it was impossible to transfer the skipper to the lifeboat, the Coxswain decided to tow the yacht to Weymouth. He took a route to avoid the Portland Race, and for a while the *Methane Princess* provided a lee by steaming alongside.

Near the Shambles Lightship, the lifeboat turned for Weymouth, and the tanker continued on passage up the Channel. With conditions a little easier, the lifeboat and the *Nomis* reached harbour at 3.30pm.

Ronald James Hardy, Coxswain and Victor Albert Charles Marsh, Second Coxswain/Mechanic, Swanage Lifeboat (both Bronze)

14 October 1976: At 1pm, the Rother class lifeboat *J. Reginald Corah* launched in a south-westerly storm force wind and very rough sea to take over the tow of the French yacht *Campscharles* from the Russian trawler *Topaz*.

Reaching the rendezvous about three miles north-east of Peveril Point, Coxswain Hardy brought the lifeboat alongside the trawler and took off two yachtsmen. In casting off the towlines, one of them fouled the lifeboat's rudder and starboard propeller. Both engines had to be stopped while an attempt to clear them was made by Second Coxswain Marsh. The rudder was cleared, and the Coxswain decided to proceed on the port engine only. One of the lifeboatmen, with a towline, was put back on the yacht which was then towed in to Poole at 4.20pm.

Victor James Pitman, Acting Coxswain, Weymouth Lifeboat (Silver)

14 October 1976: The 52 ton yacht *Latifa* was in distress off Portland Bill in a storm force south-westerly wind and worsening sea conditions. She had damaged sails, a shattered main boom, split mast and jammed halyards. A Navy frigate, acting as escort, could not take anybody off.

At 5.28pm, the Arun class lifeboat *Tony Vandervell* launched and, with the wind worsening to a hurricane and after being thrown almost on to her beam ends several times en route, she reached the yacht. A line was passed at the third attempt and Second Coxswain Pitman began the tow to Weymouth which was reached at 8.55pm.

The leadership and determination of Victor Pitman, on his second trip in command, under daunting circumstances, were inspiring and courageous. His crew, who had an average age of 50, saved eight lives under the worst conditions any of the participants could remember.

John Leslie Hodder, Helmsman and Colin Ian Jones, Crew Member, Lyme Regis Inshore Lifeboat (both Bronze)

13 August 1979: The yacht *White Kitten*, with two men, two women and a five-year-old boy on board, was lying in broken water off Beer Head; all the crew were exhausted and had been without sleep for 51 hours. Because of the heavy weather causing short, steep seas, the Atlantic 21 rigid inflatable lifeboat *U.S. Navy League*, which launched at 7.47pm, carried an extra crew member for the seven mile westward journey.

They reached the scene, and the women and the boy were transferred to the lifeboat, whilst one of the lifeboat crew (a sailing instructor) took over the yacht handling. The wind force had increased to gale, gusting storm. Helmsman Hodder landed the women and boy at Lyme Regis at 8.45pm, returned and then escorted the yacht, now being sailed by Colin Jones, safely into harbour.

Derek John Sargent, Coxswain/Mechanic, Weymouth Lifeboat (Bronze)

16 October 1987: In south-south-westerly hurricane conditions, the catamaran *Sunbeam Chaser* was reported to be stationary, under bare poles, with engine and steering problems, 12 miles south of Portland Bill.

The Arun class lifeboat *Tony Vandervell* slipped her moorings at 1.20am and forged through the adverse conditions in which she sustained damage. The *Tony Vandervell* reached the catamaran and Coxswain Sargent took her in twice to save the occupants. Refusing to acknowledge her attempts, the owner veered away each time.

Eventually three men, a woman and a youth were taken off, but the owner stayed on board. Finally he made Weymouth harbour at 9.30am in company with the lifeboat, having missed the Shambles by 100 yards. Throughout the operation the skipper ignored the lifeboat.

Christopher Haw, Coxswain, Swanage Lifeboat (Bronze)

28-29 October 1996: The relief Mersey class lifeboat *Lifetime Care* launched at 7.45pm to go to the assistance of the 90ft yacht *Be Happy* which was 22 miles from Anvil Point. She had lost her sails and one engine, and was taking water through a broken window. The wind was Force 9-11, with heavy squalls, poor visibility, and very rough seas caused by the tail-end of a hurricane.

On the way to the yacht, the lifeboat's radar went down and one engine developed problems. Aided by the searchlight of a helicopter, the lifeboat finally reached the yacht at 9.20pm. In the prevailing conditions a tow was impossible, and the yacht was drifting eastwards. The lifeboat went alongside the yacht to evacuate four crew whilst the skipper stayed at the helm.

As the two craft came together, they both rolled with such violence and speed that the lifeboat rails were crushed inboard injuring four of the lifeboatmen. One, Chris Coe, received a broken arm. Nevertheless, the four yachtsmen jumped aboard the lifeboat, followed shortly after by their skipper. The Decca Navigator on the lifeboat had now failed, and the helicopter therefore escorted the *Lifetime Care* back to Swanage arriving ten minutes after midnight. *Be Happy* subsequently went ashore on the Isle of Wight.

FOUR

Civilian Bravery

The Women of Lyme (1643), defenders of their town

Dorset has played a significant role in time of war even though no major battle has ever been fought on its soil. One perennial reason has been its forty miles of coastline and the consequent need to secure its ports, either for incoming reinforcements and supplies from the continent or, as in the case of D-Day, for outgoing invasion forces. Another was that it formed a crucial link in the Civil War between the Royalist strongholds of Exeter and Oxford, and it is from this period that the story of the Women of Lyme emerges.

As soon as the Civil War broke out in August 1642, the Parliamentary leaders in Dorset hurriedly secured the various ports along the coast. Defensive earthworks were thrown up around Lyme Regis, and in January 1643 the worst fears of the townspeople were realised when news came through that Royalist forces were approaching. In a flurry of preparation the people of Lyme laid up large stores of food and ammunition in anticipation of an attack.

On 21 April, Prince Maurice, Charles I's nephew, arrived to take the town. He looked down from the hill above and what he saw was an easy capture; 'a morning's work,' he boasted. But he had not calculated on the spirit of the defenders, especially their womenfolk.

Six weeks later, the siege was still in progress, an astonishing statistic in view of the fact that only 500 men and women were battling it out against more than five thousand soldiers. The women fired cannon and muskets from the defences, they pulled thatch from the roofs of the houses to prevent them from being set on fire by the Royalists, they put out the many fires that had already been started by them – even gathering stones to drop on the heads of Royalists trying to climb up the earthen ramparts.

By the morning of 15 June the siege was over, the Royalists having slipped away in the night. Two years later the Puritan minister, James Strong, decided to honour them in a commemorative poem, whose title alone is an indication of their bravery:

'Joaneridos; or feminine valour: Eminently discovered in Western Women: As Well By defying the merciless Enemy at the face abroad, as by fighting against them in Garrison Townes; sometimes carrying Stones, anon tumbling of stones over the Workes on the Enemy, when they have been scaling them, some carrying Powder, others charging of Peeces to ease the Souldiers, constantly resolved for generality, not to think any one life deare, to maintain that Christian quarrel for the PARLIAMENT. Whereby, as they deserve Commendations in themselves, so are they proposed as examples unto others.'

Lady Mary Bankes (1598-1661), defender of Corfe Castle

Another event in the Civil War that cannot go unremembered in the annals of heroism is Lady Mary Bankes' defence of Corfe Castle. Although she was not the only woman of her time to defend a besieged castle (take, for example, Lady Arundel of Wardour or Lady Digby of Sherborne), her gallantry and stubborn resistance to Roundhead intrusion make her story particularly remarkable.

On May Day 1643, Sir John Bankes, now Attorney-General, shortly to be promoted to Lord Chief Justice, was in Oxford with the king. Back at Corfe the traditional stag hunt was due to take place and, since there had been no sign of Civil War in Purbeck up to this poi t, Lady Bankes, as Lady of the Manor, decided to go ahead with the custom as usual.

However, the Parliamentary forces planned to gain entry to the castle under cover of the activities of the hunt. It was the practice to leave the postern gate of the castle open for the returning huntsmen and when fifty horsemen appeared, it could have been thought they were innocently returning from the chase. By a stroke of luck or good timing, Lady Bankes' own huntsmen and hunt followers appeared first, crying 'We are betrayed! Cromwell's men are upon us!' Lady Bankes' decisive response was to bar the gates, saying 'We will defend ourselves.'

And thus began a sequence of events involving an emotional mix of great courage, fine leadership, base treachery and low despair, lasting more than twenty months. In the end resistance proved futile. By the end of 1644, all of Dorset had fallen to the Parliamentary forces, with the exception of Corfe Castle, and it was only a matter of time before Corfe, too, would be taken.

It did not help that at the end of that same year Sir John was impeached by Parliament on a charge of High Treason, his wife and family were declared 'malignants' and their entire property was declared forfeit. Before the year was over, Sir John had died in Oxford, so when the expected siege was laid by Colonel Bingham in late January 1645, Lady Bankes had no husband by her side to help her defend the castle nor, in view of the impeachment, could she expect to be treated leniently by the Roundheads.

The battle for the castle was ferocious and lasted less than a month, not for lack of resolve on the part of the besiegers, but because of betrayal by a Royalist within the castle. Colonel John Pitman had requested permission to go to Somerset to raise much-needed reinforcements, but instead he went to Bingham. In return for safe conduct he agreed to lead a party of Roundheads into the castle disguised as Royalist reinforcements.

The ruse worked and the siege was over. But there were no bloody reprisals against the defenders. Colonel Bingham, a neighbour, who must have known the Bankes family well, had been extraordinarily impressed by the courage of 'Brave Dame Mary' (as she had become known) and of her followers, and he allowed all of them a safe passage out of the castle. She lived out her last days at Damory Court in Blandford and was buried at the family seat in Ruislip, Middlesex, where her tablet in Saint Martin's Church pays tribute to her qualities:

To the memory of
The Lady Mary Bankes …
of Blessed Memory
who having had the honour to have borne with
a constancy & Courage above her sex, a
noble proporcion of the Late Calamities, and
the happiness to have outlived them so farr
as to have seene the restitution of the
Government, with great peace of mind
laid down her most desired life the 11th day
of April 1661.

The 'Clubmen' (1645), history's first peace movement

We have all heard of the Tolpuddle Martyrs and their fateful clubbing together to try to ensure adequate provision for their families on starvation-level wages (*see page 59*), but less well known are the so-called 'Clubmen', who banded together two centuries earlier to protect their property from the ravages of Civil War. Royalist and Parliamentary forces alike then kept sweeping through Dorset, owing to its strategic link between London and the West of England. Untold damage was being caused to property, crops and livestock. Everybody affected was becoming sick and tired of the depredations.

The 'Clubmen' consisted of ordinary Dorset yeomen and tradesmen, along with some clergymen and a few of the gentry who were prepared to take the lead in their common plight. Their motto, displayed on banners, was:

'If you offer to plunder or take our cattle,
Be assured we will bid you battle.'

In June 1645 a meeting was held at Sturminster Newton, where 'The Humble Petition of the Distressed Inhabitants of the County of Dorset' was drawn up, demanding King and Parliament to bring an end to the fighting and a peaceful settlement to the Civil War. Wearing white cockades, they attended various mass meetings, the largest being a gathering of some four thousand on Cranborne Chase, followed by another on Badbury Rings. Although they were suing for peace, they armed themselves with clubs, swords and pitchforks for 'the mutual defence of their liberties against the plunderers and other unlawful violence.'

Two months later, Fairfax's siege of Royalist Sherborne Castle risked failure because of unwelcome interference by the Clubmen, who had succeeded in cutting off supplies to his forces and disrupting communications.

By now he had had enough of being harassed by what seemed to him like a rabble army, and he gave his Lieutenant General, Oliver Cromwell, orders to disperse them. This Cromwell did, but the Clubmen regrouped in a fortified position on Castle Hill in Shaftesbury, where Cromwell seized fifty of the ringleaders, intending to take them as prisoners to Fairfax at Sherborne.

Undaunted, 2,000 Clubmen re-gathered on Duncliffe Hill, vowing to return to Shaftesbury and rescue their leaders, but they were no match for Cromwell's trained force and they were quickly driven from the town back to Duncliffe.

Cromwell then sent a squadron of horse to ask, civilly, for someone to be sent to talk to him, but the horsemen were greeted with musket fire. However, one man, Mr Lee, came down the hill in response, and was sent back 'to desire them to peaceableness and to submit to the Parliament.'

The Clubmen would not hear of it, and fired again on Cromwell's cavalry. A second time Mr Lee was sent for to assure them that 'if they would lay down their arms no wrong should be done to them.' Still they refused, so Cromwell put them to flight.

The final episode in the drama took place on Hambledon Hill, where 3,000 Clubmen had gathered. Cromwell continued to show uncharacteristic patience and several times asked them to lay down their arms, offering to discuss their grievances.

Thomas Bravell, the Clubmen's commander, ordered his men to stand firm, threatening to 'pistol any who give back.' By now Cromwell's patience was exhausted, and he organised an attack from the rear. For a while the Clubmen held out, but in the end Cromwell overwhelmed them with his disciplined force of fifty dragoons, killing twelve and taking prisoner the three hundred who had stayed to fight. The rest scrambled down the hillside to safety.

The final humiliation came when the captured Clubmen were locked up for the night in Shroton Church. No doubt the horror of what might happen to them the next day cooled their ardour. In fact, they were given nothing more than a lecture from Cromwell, who left them in no doubt of the consequences if they misbehaved again. In his report to Fairfax, Cromwell explained that 'we have taken about 300, many of which are poor silly creatures, whom if you please to let me send home they promise to be dutiful for time to come, and will be hanged before they come out again.'

The latter threat had the desired effect, and so ended the 'Clubmen's Rebellion', the first peace movement, which for a few months became a third force in the English Civil War, and which, incidentally, gave the word 'club' (in the sense of a collection of people with a common interest) to the English language.

Ann Hutchins, rescuer of John Hutchins' *History of Dorset* in 1762
In a book about Dorset heroes perhaps Ann Hutchins deserves pride of place, yet how many have ever heard of her? Her timely and courageous actions saved for students of Dorset a unique work, without which the county's history would have been immeasurably poorer.

I am referring, of course, to John Hutchins' *History and Antiquities of the County of Dorset*. This magnificent work was the result of more than forty year's worth of scholarly research and was published in three fine editions between 1774 and 1870.

In 1762 John Hutchins, then vicar of Holy Trinity in Wareham, was away preaching in Bridport. It was a Sunday in July and the weather in the preceding weeks had been hot and dry. It was about three o'clock in the afternoon and a south-westerly breeze was blowing, when a man working at The Bull's Head in Wareham popped outside to dump some smouldering ashes on to a scrubby area of wasteland.

Within seconds the breeze had fanned the glowing embers into flames. Soon the nearby thatch was alight. Before long almost the whole of Wareham was ablaze. John Hutchins' rectory was the fourth house to catch fire, so Ann Hutchins had very little warning, but her first instinct was to save the mountain of notes being used by her husband to compile his great history.

She must have been intimately aware of which papers out of the many in his study needed to be safeguarded. If you have seen the heavyweight volumes which make up Hutchins' *History*, you will appreciate the strength required to gather up so much material – piles of manuscripts, correspondence and illustrations. She carried all of this to safety, and legend has it that she stood in the River Frome until the flames had abated and there was no chance that flying sparks would set light to her husband's precious life's work.

Sadly John Hutchins never lived to see the fruits of his labours as he died in the year before its publication, aged seventy-five. His wife must have been the product of sturdy stock, because not only did she save the *History* and a quarter of their possessions in the fire, but she went on to outlive him by more than twenty years!

The Tolpuddle Martyrs (1834), innocent victims of social injustice
George Loveless, James Loveless, James Brine, James Hammett, Thomas Standfield, John Standfield. A list of six ordinary-sounding names from the village of Tolpuddle – but what resonance for students of social history! On a cold morning in February 1834 a farm labourer left his cottage to go to work. He did not get far before he was accosted by the parish constable with the words, 'I have a warrant from the magistrates for your arrest, Mr Loveless.'

Thus began one of the biggest travesties of justice in British legal history. One arrest followed another until all six men were in the constable's custody. And what was the charge? George Loveless, the first man arrested, read the warrant, which accused him and his companions of having participated in the administration of an illegal oath. A seemingly inoffensive charge, yet the men were marched to Dorchester, stripped and searched, their heads were shorn and they were locked up like desperate criminals.

Why was such drastic action taken against humble labourers with no stain on their character? The answer is fear. The drama has to be seen against a backdrop of the times in which the men were living. The French Revolution had sent shock waves through Europe. Even forty years later, the authorities were still terrified of an uprising by the working classes. Only three years earlier a revolt stemming from discontent at the grinding poverty suffered by the peasantry had spread throughout the south. In Dorset, ricks were burned and machinery was smashed. The revolt was crushed and intelligent working men realised that the way forward was through peaceful political action, not rioting.

The repeal of the Combination Laws in 1824 had removed the penalties for belonging to a Trade Union. Workers in the countryside saw in Trades Unionism a means of alleviating the distress and poverty resulting from their appallingly low wages. The labourers in Tolpuddle, under the leadership of George Loveless, had met and determined to demand the same wages as were paid in other parts of Dorset, namely ten shillings a week. With the help of the vicar an agreement was reached, but then, inexplicably, their farmer employers reneged and would pay no more than nine shillings a week.

The dissatisfaction that ensued led to retaliatory action by the farmers, who reduced the wages to eight shillings. George Loveless went to see the magistrates trusting that they would see justice done, but returned rebuffed by a ruling that the farmers could not be compelled to pay more than they wished. Determined to give their employees a salutary lesson, the farmers now reduced the wages to seven shillings with the threat of a further reduction to six shillings.

A key moment in the drama had been reached and it was only then that the labourers began to combine. As ever George Loveless took the lead (he was an eloquent preacher in the local Wesleyan Methodist Church, a man of great natural ability and strength of character). With the help of two delegates from London representing the Grand National Consolidated Trades Union, the men established the 'Friendly Society of Agricultural Labourers' at Tolpuddle. Trades Unionism had come to Dorset.

The rest of the story is well known. The men were tried and sentenced to seven years' transportation. They suffered further degradations in the prison hulks at Portsmouth, on board the ships sailing to Tasmania and Botany Bay and in the harsh penal colonies. Their families at home shared in their punishment and were, effectively, sentenced to starvation, being denied parish relief on the grounds that if they could afford to pay a penny a week to support the unions then they needed no further assistance. Agitation for the release of the Tolpuddle Six became so great that after two years the men were pardoned. All but James Hammet settled in Ontario in Canada. Hammett returned to his native Tolpuddle and is buried in the village.

The final word on the injustice of their case lies in George Loveless's statement made at the end of the trial before verdict was pronounced. When Judge John Williams asked if the defendants had anything to say, George Loveless passed him a sheet of writing, whereupon the Judge asked him whether he wished this to be read out in court. When Loveless signalled in the affirmative, the Judge mumbled the statement inaudibly to the Jury to the extent that Loveless himself could not understand it. These were the telling words the Jury did not hear:

'My Lord, if we have violated any law, it was not done intentionally; we have injured no man's reputation, character, person, or property: we were uniting together to preserve ourselves, our wives and our children, from utter degradation and starvation. We challenge any man, or number of men, to prove that we have acted, or intended to act, different from the above statement.'

George Vince (1880-1902), polar explorer

George Vince was born in Blandford and lived at his father's fish shop at 83 Salisbury Street. He took up Boy Service in the Royal Navy (at a boyish height of 5ft 1in) on a twelve year engagement.

In October 1901 he joined Captain Scott's Antarctic Expedition at Cape Town as a seaman on *Discovery*, and by February 1902 the ship was anchored at McMurdo Sound.

The following month the crews set out in teams, sledging with dogs. Returning from Mount Crozier, Vince's group was hauling sledges up a steep slope and encountered a blizzard at the top. They pitched tent and had some cold food. The cookers were all out of order and the men had had no hot food that day. The tents were badly pitched, they had no furs on, the cold was intense, some of the men were frost-bitten and all of them were exhausted.

To make matters worse, Vince was coughing up blood. He had also changed into fur boots, instead of the spiked boots the others were wearing, to ease the pain in his sore feet. This would prove to be his undoing.

A furious blizzard was blowing and visibility was down to five yards. The group's leader, Barne, decided to strike camp and return to the ship. As they made their way back they suddenly came upon an ice slope and the entire group of five started to slide down uncontrollably. Fortunately for four of them, there were snow banks into which they could dig in with their spikes and halt their descent.

Unbeknown to any of them, there was an ice cliff further down. Vince, in his fur boots, was completely unable to stop and hurtled towards the edge, plummeted downwards and plunged into the icy sea, where death would have been swift in the sub-zero temperatures.

Shocked and dismayed the others climbed back up, calling on their last reserves of strength and using knives to aid their purchase on the ice. On their return to the *Discovery* they told their story to Scott, who in 1904 erected a cross to Vince's memory at Hut Point on Ross Island.

Repaired in 1987, the cross is still there, at 77°50'S, 166°37E', commemorating the boy from Blandford who died a world away from home, during one of the most famous periods of Polar exploration, in the icy wastes of the Antarctic.

FIVE

Sporting Prowess

Robert Montagu Poore (1866-1938),
outstanding batsman of his generation

Brigadier-General Robert Montagu Poore was, by any standards, a man who stood out from the crowd. At 6ft 4in tall, he had a formidable appearance, and, as commanding officer of one of the British Army's great cavalry regiments, the 7th Hussars, he served alongside some of the most notable names in military history – Kitchener, Roberts and Haig. But this was only part of the story.

It was his sporting prowess that made him a legend, and he has been variously described as 'one of the most remarkable athletes of his time' and 'one of the outstanding batsmen of his generation'. His biography by Jeremy Lonsdale calls him, quite simply, *The Army's Grace.*

Apart from his skill with the cricket bat playing for Hampshire, he was reckoned to be the finest English swordsman and horseman of his era. He was also a superb polo player at a time when the game was an imperial obsession, and elsewhere he won numerous tennis, squash and shooting competitions.

However, in what has been called the 'Golden Age of Batting', it was Poore's skill at the wicket that caught the imagination of the public. For a considerable time no one had a better average in an English season (1899) than his 91.23, until Don Bradman bettered it in 1930. To this day, the English sixth wicket partnership record is still 411 by R. M. Poore and E. G. Wynyard, made in just over four hours, in July 1899, against Somerset at Taunton. Poore's score of 304 stood as a Hampshire record until R. H. Moore beat it in 1937, and it is still the county's second highest innings. A further record was set on that day. The 411 was a large proportion of the highest number of runs scored in one day at that time – 606 in all. Poore had batted for six hours and fifty minutes, reaching his 300 ten minutes earlier.

Add to this his glorious June of 1899, and you begin to see what forged Poore's sporting reputation. During the space of a single fortnight, he made the winning hit in the final of the Inter-Regimental Polo Tournament at Hurlingham, won the title of Best Man at Arms at the Royal Naval and Military Tournament, and, to cap it all, he scored three centuries in a row for Hampshire in the County Championship.

Poore's connection with Dorset began in 1921, when he retired from the Army, just five days before his fifty-fifth birthday, and settled down to an active life on an Army pension at the Manor House, Hinton St Mary.

From 1921 he turned out for his local side, Hinton St Mary United in the Ranston Cricket League. He laid out a wicket at his home and constructed what he referred to as the 'gibbet', a frame with a suspended ball where he could practise his strokes. He gave local boys, and children of visiting friends, instruction in his garden, or explained batting technique to them indoors using photographs. In his absence, it was not unknown for his wife, Lady Flora, sister of the Duke of Hamilton, to give occasional coaching lessons.

Poore began to give more time to his golf, becoming a low handicap player at Broadstone, as well as playing at the Ranelagh Club in London, or at Sandwich in Kent. In 1923-24 he played for Dorset Golf Club, the Cavalry Club and Dorset Amateurs. He ultimately captained Broadstone Golf Club.

In 1926 Poore moved to a new home, Rose Lawn Coppice, Merley, near Wimborne. Here he was quickly recruited by Broadstone Cricket Club, making 56 and 53 not out in his early innings.

In the spring of 1927 Poore established what was to become a regular feature of the remaining years of his life – the Easter coaching classes in Bournemouth, designed to help develop local cricket talent. Two years later Bournemouth Cricket Club had expanded to take in squash, tennis, golf and rugby, and in 1930 became the Bournemouth Cricket and Sports Club Limited, with Poore as one of its first directors.

The highlight of the club's 1930 season came with opening of the new ground by Poore. It was his honour, as Club President, to cut the silk stretched across the wicket, and then he led out the Gentlemen of Hampshire against the Gentlemen of Dorset in a fixture which had not been played for twenty years.

In March 1931 he played for the English Senior Golfers Society, and in April he won the Bournemouth foursomes final with Captain A.V. Hambro MP. He also came eighth in the Dorset Amateur Golf Championship.

In 1931 he became President of the Bournemouth branch of the South African War Veterans Association (Poore had served in South Africa in 1895 with his regiment, and had played in three Test Matches for South Africa against England).

Poore died in 1938, and was buried in his back garden in a grave consecrated by the Bishop of Salisbury. Lady Flora followed him twenty years later, and they lie side by side overlooking Broadstone Golf Course.

Charles Bennett (1870-1949),
Britain's first Olympic track & field gold medallist

In 1900, at the dawn of a new century, Charles Bennett was a 29-year-old engine driver living in the village of his birth, Shapwick, but he was a driver with a difference, because, before the year was out, he had secured a place for himself in sporting history.

As one of the top British middle distance runners of his generation, he had already won the AAA mile championship in 1897, and the cross country title in 1899 and 1900. In the latter year, also the Olympic year, he won the British title in the mile, thus qualifying for the 1,500 metres at the Paris Olympics.

Bennett led throughout the race, beating local favourite Henri Deloge by four tenths of a second, setting a new world record of 4 minutes 6.2 seconds, and making history by winning Britain's first track and field Olympic gold.

Bennett won a second Olympic title in the 5,000 metres team event, breaking another world record, albeit unofficial, in a time of 15 minutes 29.2 seconds. He was also part of the British clean sweep of medals in the 4,000 metres steeplechase.

Bennett's astonishing double world record took the British public by storm, and he was fêted on his return home, but continued to work as an engine driver, later retiring to run the Dolphin pub (now Gulliver's Tavern) at Kinson. He died in Bournemouth in 1949, aged 78.

In 2004, another great Olympic year of medals for Britain, Bennett's grandson and fellow residents of Shapwick decided to honour his

ABOVE Coxswain Alfred Pavey (second from left) posing outside the Royal Festival Hall in 1973 prior to the presentation of his medal, which he won for towing a tanker to safety off Portland (see page 49).

BELOW Helmsman John Hodder (left) and Crew Member Colin Jones (right) of the Lyme Regis Inshore Lifeboat were awarded bronze medals in 1979 for the dramatic rescue of a yacht off Beer Head. This was Hodder's second medal; his first was won in 1971 when he dived into the sea off Lyme Regis to save a fisherman's son from drowning (see pages 49 & 51).

LEFT Lady Mary Bankes, 'Brave Dame Mary', held Corfe Castle against Roundhead troops for more than twenty months, finally capitulating because of treachery. This imposing statue of her can be seen at Kingston Lacy House (see page 54).

BELOW The Tolpuddle Martyrs Memorial, sculpted from local Portland stone by Tom Dagnall, was unveiled in 2001, and stands in front of the Martyrs Cottages in Tolpuddle. The life-size stone figure of George Loveless expresses the anguish of the martyrs' desperate situation in 1824 (see page 59).

Four sportsmen associated with Dorset.
TOP LEFT The cricketer Robert Montague Poore (see page 62).
TOP RIGHT Athlete Charles Bennett, who won Britain's first track and field gold medal at the 1900 Paris Olympics (see page 64).
BELOW LEFT Came Down golfer Reginald ('R.A.') Whitcombe, winner of the 1938 Open at Sandwich (see page 67).
BELOW RIGHT Freddie Mills, the World Light-Heavyweight boxing champion of 1948 (see page 68).

Former Weymouth College pupil and Schneider Cup aviator George Stainforth being chaired in triumph by the College OTC after his record-breaking flight in 1931. Stainforth was the first man in history to fly at more than 400 miles per hour. The photograph below shows him in the Vickers' Supermarine Rolls-Royce S6-B that powered him to his record (see page 65).

RIGHT Poole-based Rodney Pattisson made Olympic sailing history when he won his third medal in succession at the 1976 Olympics. He has continued to have a strong influence on the sport, and his book, *Tactics*, is still regarded as one of the definitive works on the subject (see page 71).

BELOW Jubilant scenes at Wembley Stadium in 1992 after Wimborne Town Football Club had achieved the seemingly impossible task of winning the FA Vase (see page 72).

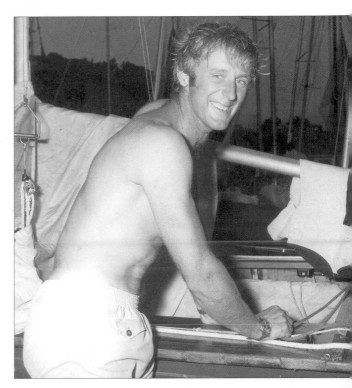

ABOVE LEFT 17th century
physician Thomas Sydenham,
'Father of modern medicine', was
well ahead of his time with his
views of how disease should be
treated (see page 75).

ABOVE RIGHT Robert Boyle of
Stalbridge gave his name to one of
chemistry's most famous laws,
'Boyle's Law'. He helped found
The Royal Society, the oldest
continuing scientific society in the
world (see page 76).

LEFT Unsung pioneer of
vaccination, Benjamin Jesty was a
country farmer who inoculated his
family against smallpox twenty-
two years before Edward Jenner
performed his first inoculation (see
page 77).

ABOVE LEFT Dubbed the 'British Audubon', John Gould created a priceless heritage of fine bird-paintings after a lifetime spent collecting specimens and illustrating them in his famous monographs. The most popular plates from his books are those of the brightly-coloured hummingbirds (see page 80).

ABOVE RIGHT Alfred Russel Wallace, who made Dorset his home, was a giant in the world of nineteenth century natural history, working alongside Charles Darwin on his theories of evolution. He is buried in Broadstone Cemetery underneath a free-standing fossilised tree trunk (see page 82).

RIGHT Sir Frederick Treves achieved popular fame when he befriended Joseph Merrick, the 'Elephant Man', but he was a thoroughly dedicated surgeon who made a special study of appendicitis. He loved his native Dorset, and 1906 saw the publication of his book, *Highways and Byways of Dorset*, still sought after today for its charming and accurate descriptions of the county (see page 84).

ABOVE Generally best remembered for her discovery of the first fossil *ichthyosaur*, Mary Anning was born in Lyme Regis and came from a humble background (see page 79).

RIGHT Marie Stopes, seen here in 1901 when the youngest Doctor of Science in Britain. Stopes campaigned tirelessly for women, in particular trying to change people's attitudes to contraception. She set up the first birth control clinic in Britain, and her dream of free contraception for all British women was realised in 1975. She was also a great benefactor to Portland, giving to the Island the cottages that are now Portland Museum (see page 87).

memory by raising £50,000 to buy a half-acre plot from the National Trust for a village green, to be dedicated as the Charles Bennett Memorial Field.

Now a precious piece of Olympic history lives on in Dorset for all to enjoy. A century or so after his grandfather's great achievement, grandson Chris Bennett's description of him strikes a chord, recalling all the qualities of a true Olympian: 'He had a real Corinthian spirit and ran just for the love of it. He is one of this country's unsung sporting heroes.'

George Stainforth (1899-1942), aviator and 1931 world speed record holder

In 1931, the Royal Aero Club of Britain was competing for the Schneider Cup for the third time in a row (1927, 1929 and 1931), giving the event particular piquancy – if the team won (of which George Stainforth, alumnus of Weymouth College, was a member), then, under the terms of Schneider's original rules, they would gain outright possession of the trophy for the first time in the history of the competition.

The Schneider Cup was named after its creator, Jacques Schneider, a French industrialist, who believed that seaplanes were the future of civil aviation. Believing that a race specifically for seaplanes would encourage improvements in their design, in 1912 he offered a trophy whose official title was 'Coupe d'Aviation Maritime Jacques Schneider'. Less formally, the competition came to be known under various names: the Schneider Trophy, the Schneider Cup, or even 'Flying Flirt', owing to Frenchman E. Gabard's design for the trophy. The silver-plated bronze, now on display at the Science Museum in London, is a sensuous depiction of the Spirit of Flight kissing the waves, symbolising the speed of the aircraft in the air and on the water.

At 4.18pm on Sunday 13 September 1931, flying a Rolls-Royce, 2,300 horsepower Vickers Supermarine S6-B, Flight Lieutenant Stainforth began his attempt to break the world speed record, then standing at 357.7 miles per hour, set at the 1929 Schneider Cup race.

The course was a measured three kilometres between Hill Head and Lee-on-Solent Pier, and the adjudged speed would be an average of four consecutive runs over that distance. Stainforth's speciality was the 'high speed turn' – he could withstand G-forces greater than other

65

pilots, earning himself the nickname 'Cast-Iron' Stainforth.

The huge crowd watching the race were waiting for some spectacular aerobatics and were not disappointed. The rules of the competition permitted a dive on to the course as steep as the competitor's machine would stand, allowing time to flatten out before entering the measured sector. Stainforth began a six-mile run-up, gradually opening up to full throttle, delaying his descent from a height of 1,200 feet until the last possible moment. With the engine roaring, he turned the nose down at a steep angle, right over his mark. Spectators gasped as he pulled out of the dive at around 160 feet above the water and shot through the 'starting gate'. His flying on the best runs could not have been better done. His fastest lap was his second, when he hurtled down the Hampshire coast, with the wind behind him, at a speed of 388.67mph, the fastest a plane had ever travelled in aviation history.

The following day the times were ratified, eliminating stop-watch error, and Stainforth's mean of the four runs, submitted to the FAI (Fédération Aéronautique Internationale), was 379.05 miles per hour. The Royal Aero Club of Britain was now the three times winner of the Schneider Trophy.

Extraordinarily, this was not the end of Stainforth's speed record attempts. A fortnight later at Calshot, in a more powerful machine, he raised the record to an astonishing 408.8mph, including a run of 415mph, becoming the first man in the world to exceed a speed of 400 miles per hour in an aircraft.

On 9 October 1931 Stainforth was awarded the Air Force Cross by King George V. Rising through the ranks to Wing-Commander, he was appointed Officer in Command of No. 89 Squadron, posted to the Middle East in December 1941. There, whilst piloting a Beaufighter, near the Gulf of Suez, Stainforth was killed in action on the night of 27-28 September 1942, aged 43, eleven years almost to the day after his record flight. He was buried with full military honours at the British Cemetery, Ismailia, Egypt.

In addition to his world speed records, he had successes in King's Cup Races, and he held the Upside Down Flight Record of 11 minutes 57 seconds. His career sheet was no less impressive, showing 4,773 flying hours, including 961 hours of experimental flying for RAF Farnborough.

George Hedley Stainforth was a fine airman, who knew no fear and who competed at a time when exceptional technical difficulties went hand in hand with ever-present danger, because of the limits to which flying skills were being pushed.

Crowds in excess of 250,000 spectators gathered to watch the Schneider Cup races, evidence of keen public interest in this type of competition. The seaplanes were indisputably beautiful flying machines, but it was the pilots who were the heroes of the day.

Reginald Whitcombe (1898-1957), 1938 Open golf champion

Reginald Whitcombe was a natural golfer, who holds the distinction of being one of only two players from the South-West of England to have won the Open Championship. The other was J. H. Taylor, who was born close to the famous links of Westward Ho!, and who won the 1894 Open at Sandwich, the first time it had been played outside Scotland.

Whitcombe was the youngest of three famous golfing brothers, Ernest, Charles and Reginald, who were associated with Came Down Golf Club, near Weymouth. All three achieved prominence between the two World Wars, and it was anybody's guess as to which of them would be the victor in any given tournament.

Having been outshone by Ernest (the Came Down professional) and Charles in his early years, Reginald had shown, in 1922, that he could beat his two elder brothers on his home course. In the 1924 Western Counties Championship the brothers took first, second and third place.

Reginald had begun to show his paces in a wider field. One astute journalist noted that 'Reginald is a sound and capable golfer who, blessed with just a little luck, may some day be rubbing shoulders in the higher walks of golf with the rest of the family.' This was a prophetic remark, for over the next few years he won many significant tournaments, including, in 1936, the Irish Open Championship, having been runner-up the previous year.

In 1935 all three brothers played in the Great Britain Ryder Cup team, and Charles' record of having played in every Ryder Cup match between 1927 and 1937 is unsurpassed.

In the 1937 Open Championship Reginald was runner-up to Henry Cotton at Carnoustie, and his victory in the 1938 Open at Sandwich was accomplished in the most testing conditions ever known. Gale force winds swept across the course, so that the least error brought disaster. It was a tremendous test of stamina, and Reginald, used to the windswept terrain of Came Down, was the man for the task.

His win was a popular one, as a win by any of the three brothers would have been. His book, *R. A. Whitcombe Says Golf's No Mystery!*, was published in 1938, reprinted twice, and went into a third impression in 1939. In it, he stressed that golf is 'a natural game', that 'simple straightforward hitting of the ball' is the key to success, and (an advanced idea for the time) that 'controlled breathing' makes the player 'master of himself', overcoming the 'nervous tension which spoils the chances of so many players.' I defy any golfer to deny that strikes a chord!

In 1928, Reginald Whitcombe left Came Down to become the professional at Parkstone Golf Club, where he remained until his death in 1957.

The Whitcombe brothers' contribution to golf remains unsurpassed by any members of a single family. Between them they won every prize in a game upon which, individually and collectively, they had the finest possible influence.

Freddie Mills (1919-1965),
World Light-Heavyweight boxing champion

Born in Terrace Road, Bournemouth in June 1919, Freddie Mills used to train in a back room behind the Cricketer's Arms in Holdenhurst Road, where he worked behind the bar. He went to St Michael's School, was once a Malmesbury & Parsons milkman, and started his boxing career under the Parkstone promoter, Jack Turner. His first fights were at the Winter Gardens in Bournemouth.

His professional career spanned fourteen years, from 1936 to 1950, during which time he achieved all the titles open to him in the light-heavyweight class. His record is still unrivalled – in a total of 97 bouts, he scored 75 wins, 17 losses and 5 draws. If you exclude the draws, exactly half of those matches ended in a knock-out.

His first major success came in June 1942 when he beat Len Harvey in a second round knock-out to win the Commonwealth and British light-heavyweight titles. Two years later, he lost those titles to Jack London in Manchester, but the fight went the full fifteen rounds.

His first attempt at the world title was in 1946, when he boxed against titleholder Gus Lesnevich. Mills, however, was knocked out in the tenth round and Lesnevich retained his title. He took Lesnevich on again for the world title in July 1948 in London, taking it the full fifteen rounds. This was Mills' crowning achievement – he won the title, and was now World Light-Heavyweight Boxing Champion, at the age of twenty-nine.

In the intervening two years Mills had boxed Pol Goffaux in London, in September 1947, with a knock-out in the second round, to take the European title, successfully defending the same title in February 1948, defeating Paco Bueno.

Mills held on to his world title for another two years, losing to Joey Maxim in 1950 after a knock-out in the tenth round, but retaining his legendary status as a boxer in the public eye.

For years, Mills was in huge demand, both on radio and television. He wrote a boxing column for a Sunday newspaper, did some acting, including roles in two *Carry On* films, became a friend of Sid James and Bob Monkhouse, and in partnership with former actor Andy Ho, he opened one of London's first Chinese restaurants.

But tragedy struck in 1965 when he was found dead on the back seat of his car, just yards from the restaurant, which by then had been converted into a nightclub. He had been shot once in the head; the rifle rested between his knees. The coroner recorded a verdict of suicide, but to this day there are some who believe that Mills was not a man to commit suicide, and that he was murdered.

We shall never know the answer, but what remains undisputed is that Freddie Mills was one of Britain's best-loved sporting figures, a hero to millions, and a courageous man, who was the greatest light-heavyweight boxer of his generation.

Sam Rockett (1919-1989), cross-Channel swimmer

Sam Rockett was one of nine finishers out of twenty-four competitors in the first *Daily Mail* International Channel Race of 1950, Cap Gris Nez to England, and was the first Briton home.

He performed in what might be called the 'Golden Age of Cross-Channel Swimming'. In the 1950s and 60s, swims were front page news – they were broadcast live on TV and radio, and were shown on the Pathé News in cinemas.

Rockett's swimming career began in the prestigious Poole Swimming Club, which produced many champions over the years. Born in Milborne St Andrew in 1919, Rockett moved with his family to Poole in 1925 when he was six years old. Showing early talent as a swimmer, he went on to become a well known water polo player, competing for Dorset and several other counties.

Following his Channel swim, Rockett resigned from his job with ICI, and took up the post of Assistant Manager at the Folkestone open-air swimming pool. He was also invited to be the Training Supervisor and Technical Adviser for the second *Daily Mail* Race in 1951. The race was marred by an international incident which blew up when the Egyptians refused their prizes on the grounds that the *Daily Mail* had slandered the King of Egypt. The huge publicity that the event attracted kept it in the public eye, and Rockett went on to write *It's Cold in the Channel* (1956). The book gives excellent coverage of Channel swimming up to the mid-1950s, and is essential background reading and early reference material for the serious Channel swimmer.

In 1957 a London company, Eros Films, released *Stormy Crossing*, a who-dunnit about the murder of a cross-Channel swimmer, set in Dover and Folkestone, and starring John Ireland, Derek Bond and Leslie Dwyer. Rockett featured in a bit-part in the film and was technical adviser, but for some film buffs *Stormy Crossing*'s chief claim to fame is that the Dover garage owner was played by Arthur Lowe of *Dad's Army* renown.

Folkestone Pool closed in 1959, but Rockett continued to train Channel swimmers until about 1964. A number of those in his squad achieved success, such as Godfrey Chapman and Antonio Abertondo, who, in 1961, was the first man to swim both ways non-stop.

For the rest of his life, until his death in Folkestone in 1989, Rockett was regarded as a swimming guru, and his huge knowledge and experience were consulted, amongst others, by the BBC, the press and even Hollywood film directors.

In 1983 Poole swimmer Samantha Druce earned a place in the *Guinness Book of Records* as the youngest person to swim the Channel. She completed the crossing in 15 hours 26 minutes at the age of 12 years 118 days. She remains the youngest girl to complete the crossing.

Rodney Pattisson (born 1943), Olympic yachtsman

Poole yachtsman and Royal Marine Rodney Pattisson established himself as Britain's most successful Olympic sailor when he won medals in the Flying Dutchman class at three consecutive Olympic games: a gold at Acapulco in 1968, another gold in the 1972 games at Kiel, and finally a silver in Montreal in 1976.

Nearly thirty years later his record has still not been overtaken, although it was equalled at the 2004 Olympics, when Ben Ainslie, from neighbouring Hampshire, took gold in the Laser class at Athens, having won silver in Atlanta in 1996, and gold in Sydney in 2000.

Pattisson's passion for sailing began when his family moved to Swanage when he was only seven years old. There he helped his father, Lieutenant-Commander Kenneth Pattisson (see page 30), build the family Cadet (he still has it). His father then taught his four children how to sail, introducing the boat to Swanage Sailing Club, where a Cadet class was formed.

Pattisson went to Forres Preparatory School in Swanage, followed by Pangbourne Nautical College, joining Dartmouth as a Cadet in 1961. The previous year he had achieved his first real sailing success, winning the Cadet National Championships at Burnham on Crouch.

During his competitive sailing career, Pattisson amassed an impressive portfolio of sailing achievements. He won the Flying Dutchman World Championships three times, and the European Championships four. He also did a considerable amount of big boat sailing, including the Admiral's Cup, Fastnet and Hobart.

In 1979 he sailed with the Irish Admiral's Cup team in the Fastnet, aboard *Golden Apple*, and was on the winning boat *Jade* in the One Ton World Championships held at Poole in 1986.

In 1983 Pattisson co-skippered, with Lawrie Smith, the 12-metre yacht *Victory '83* in Peter de Savary's challenge for the America's Cup, getting further than any other British challenge, reaching the final of the Louis Vuitton Cup, only to be beaten by the radical Australian boat *Australia II*, which went on to win against Dennis Connor's *Liberty*.

Resigning his commission in 1971, after 10 years specialising as a submariner, he started his own company, importing 470 Olympic Class dinghies built in Spain. Later he imported the early windsurfers, and, later still, folding trailer-trimarans built in the United States.

He wrote the definitive book, *Tactics*, on the skills required to outmanoeuvre the rest of the fleet, with sections on match racing, team racing, off-wind starts and racing near the shore. He now lectures on 'the Olympics before Professionalism'.

Pattisson celebrated his sixtieth year in unusual style by marrying a local girl (one of his biggest fans, whom he had only recently met) in the twelfth century St Aldhelm's Chapel, which perches on the windswept cliff tops of Purbeck. He sailed to the ceremony in his trimaran, anchoring in Chapman's Pool and climbing the cliff to the chapel.

At the reception, at Harry Warren House, Studland, an old Flying Dutchman of Pattisson's was on show beside his original Cadet, a memento of his first forays into the sport which he served (and continues to serve) so well.

Wimborne Town Football Club, FA Vase winners 1992

In 2003 Wimborne Town Football Club celebrated its 125th anniversary. But to learn about the zenith of the club's history we have to go back eleven years earlier, to 1992.

Wimborne Town Football Club's most glorious moment was undoubtedly in that triumphal year, when they achieved an extraordinary triple success by not only finishing the season as the Jewson Wessex League champions *and* capturing the Dorset Senior Cup without conceding a single goal, but, most remarkable of all, attaining the giddy heights of reaching, and winning, the final of the FA Vase at Wembley Stadium in a match described by the Football Association as 'the best Vase Final in the history of the competition'.

The FA Vase is the equivalent of the FA Cup for teams excluding the Premiership League, the Championship League and Divisions 1 & 2, and was instituted in 1974 when the Football Association abolished the distinction between professional and amateur status.

For Wimborne Town and the Club's fans the journey to Wembley was a roller-coaster ride. The first round result was a close 2-1 against Mangotsfield away (Richardson and Allan scoring); the second round was a more comfortable 5-2 victory against Chard Town at home (Sturgess, Allan, Richardson, Lynn, Killick); the third round, against Horsham at home, was another close result, 1-0, Sturgess scoring the only goal.

Now the fun began. Billed the 'Battle of Hastings', the fourth round match was against Hastings Town at home: score 3-3 after extra time (Killick, Richardson, Allan). The replay, away, was yet another close result: 2-1 after extra time (Lynn, Turner). Then Newcastle Town away: result, drew 1-1 after extra time (Allan). Another replay, at home: result, won 1-0, Sturgess again scoring the only goal.

By now the players must have been thinking, Can our luck last? Diss Town away was next: result, drew 0-0 after extra time (that was the fourth time in five matches). A third replay, at home: result, won 1-0, Allan scoring – the third single-goal result so far. Was the nail-biting at an end? Not a bit of it.

Semi-final first leg v. Bamber Bridge away; result 0-0. Semi-final second leg v. Bamber Bridge at home: result 2-0 (Ames scored both).

Wembley beckoned in a final against Guiseley. There on the glorious turf of one of the world's most famous stadiums, Guiseley opened the account. Nothing daunted, Richardson put in a long range shot to equalise. Two more before half time (Sturgess and Killick) put the interval score at 3-1. What could stop them now?

Guiseley pulled back a goal shortly after the restart, but then it was another one for Killick. In his book *Wimborne Minster, 1992*, Alan Bennett takes up the story: 'By now our heroes were Colossi bestriding the Wembley turf. In goal Kevin Leonard was playing with such cool anticipation and agility he inspired the players in front of him.'

When Sturgess put in Wimborne's fifth (and his second of the match), it crowned a glorious afternoon (even though Guiseley, to their credit, put in a third). As Bennett puts it: 'What more can a striker do than score twice at Wembley?' A rhetorical question? Certainly. But if one were to give an answer, perhaps Jimmy Sturgess' service to Wimborne Town Football Club exceeds even his two-goal feat at Wembley. On his retirement at the end of the 2004 season, he had played more than 600 matches for his club.

Wimburnians turned out in their hundreds to welcome their heroes in the town Square, and watched as their Mayor, Councillor Anthony Oliver, held aloft the FA Vase, surrounded by the team, their gallant victory still fresh in their memory. But take note – with the demise of the old twin-domed stadium, their record of the highest scoring Vase Final at that venue stands for all time.

Science and Medicine

Francis Glisson (1597-1677), pioneering physician
From humble roots in a small Dorset village, Francis Glisson rose to become one of the great medical men of his age. He was born in Rampisham, and was educated at the village school, finally going to Caius College, Cambridge, steadily climbing the academic ladder until in 1636 he was elected to the Regius Professorship of Physic at Cambridge. A few years later he moved to Colchester, building up a highly successful practice, as well as a solid reputation as a physician.

In 1648 he was briefly caught up in the Civil War when Colchester was besieged by Parliament and his services as a mediator were called upon. His own house was spared, but many others were destroyed. The town fell on hard times and Glisson moved to London. There, as an unmarried man with no family responsibilities, he was able to devote a large part of his time to the study of disease, in particular the so-called 'New Disease' of rickets.

On his visits to his native Dorset he saw the prevalence of rickets in the young, noting the enlarged joints and misshapen bones which were the symptoms of the disease. Today we know the cause to be lack of vitamin D, but in the mid-seventeenth century vitamins were unknown. Glisson spent five years studying the disease and correctly attributed the condition to incorrect diet. In 1650 he wrote his most famous book, *A Treatise on Rickets*. Three hundred and fifty years later, little can be added to his summing up of the pathology of the disease.

As Glisson's reputation grew, he became more and more involved with the work of the College of Physicians, becoming President from 1667 to 1669. He was one of the elite group who held meetings for the 'Promotion of Enquiries into Natural and Experimental Philosophy', leading directly to the establishment of The Royal Society, of which he was one of the first Fellows. Another founding member from Dorset was the chemist Robert Boyle.

First and foremost a physician and anatomist, Glisson embarked on his next important book, *Anatomia Hepatis*, describing in great detail the structure of the liver. The fibrous sheath in which the liver is contained is known to this day as 'Glisson's Capsule'. At the age of seventy-five Glisson produced a final, learned anatomical treatise called *Tractatus de Ventriculo et Intestinis*, based on his lectures and dedicated to the University of Cambridge and the College of Physicians.

He died in 1677 and was buried at the Church of St Bride's, Fleet Street. Thus the man who started his life in an obscure Dorset village became one of the nation's outstanding medical scientists, making a lasting contribution to the study of rickets and the liver.

Thomas Sydenham (1624-1689), father of modern medicine

Sydenham was born in the Manor House at Wynford Eagle in 1624 to a family who played a prominent part in the Civil War, one of them becoming Governor of Weymouth.

By the age of eighteen Thomas Sydenham had matriculated at Oxford, where he was strongly influenced by the Puritan movement in the city. He returned to Dorset in 1642 to fight for Parliament and Commonwealth. Two of his brothers were killed at Weymouth, and he himself was numbered among the dead, until he was found wounded on the battlefield.

Returning to Oxford in 1647, he enrolled in the Faculty of Medicine at Wadham College. He went on to build up a fine medical practice in Westminster, basing his medical techniques on the teaching of Hippocrates.

His first book, a treatise in Latin on fevers, had considerable impact, and he gained a reputation, at home and abroad, for his observations on epidemic diseases, the cooling method of treating smallpox and the use of quinine.

It has to be remembered that at this time in the history of medicine, disease was still being approached by astrological and mathematical methods. Sydenham was determined to banish superstition, basing his own medical practice on careful observation of symptoms, leading to correct diagnosis.

He was sceptical about the practice of bleeding, preferring to advocate fresh air in the sick room. With calm logic he developed a set of working methods which stood him in good stead: study the symptoms; work with, not against nature; combine medical knowledge with common sense; prescribe rest, good cheer, patience and courage rather than drugs; pay careful attention to diet.

Two centuries later the renowned Dorset-born surgeon, Sir Frederick Treves (*see page 84*), would pay tribute to Sydenham, saying that he 'threw aside jargon and ridiculous traditions with which medicine was then hampered and applied to it sound common sense.'

Sydenham finally fell prey to an acute attack of gout, a disease from which he had chronically suffered and to which he had devoted some of his study. He died at his house in Pall Mall in 1689, but not before he had made an incalculable contribution to the progress of practical medical methodology, as well as publishing five invaluable works in various branches of medicine.

Robert Boyle (1627-1691), father of chemistry

Loud claps of thunder woke young Robert Boyle. The furious Alpine storm made him wonder if the Day of Judgement had arrived. If it had, was his soul ready? At that moment, the 13-year-old Boyle resolved to live a life dedicated to serving Christ, and the next fifty years were proof of his conversion.

Boyle was born in Lismore, Ireland, the youngest of fourteen, whose father, Richard Boyle, 1st Earl of Cork, was one of the wealthiest men in the British Isles. Robert Boyle was educated accordingly, first at Eton and later travelling the continent with a tutor. He learned philosophy, religion, languages, mathematics and, perhaps most significantly, the new physics of Bacon, Descartes and Galileo.

Boyle returned from his continental tour in 1644, aged 17, and settled in Stalbridge Park, the neglected estate left to him by his father. Much of the early part of this Stalbridge period was spent in moral philosophy and there was at this stage no reason to think that he would become one of the great natural philosophers of his time.

Around 1649, Boyle began to be interested in experimenting, but was hindered by the fact that he could not obtain a furnace. Those he ordered tended to arrive 'crumbled into as many pieces, as we into sects,' leaving Boyle to attempt 'such experiments, as the unfurnishedness of the place, and the present distractedness of my mind, will permit me.' Despite these difficulties, his numerous experiments resulted in major scientific reports. Today he is best known for the law bearing his name – 'Boyle's Law' – which states that the pressure of a gas is in inverse proportion to the volume that it occupies.

Boyle considered his scientific experiments, like all his other endeavours, as part of his Christian service. He believed that the orderliness of the universe reflected God's purposeful design. Ironically philosophers and scientists would later use his ideas on the mechanistic nature of the universe to remove God from its workings, but Boyle himself never thought of the universe as an autonomous machine.

His scientific studies included work on the theory of colours, respiration, gems and porosity. Many of his writings were decidedly theological. He wrote tracts on divine love, ethics, the evils of swearing, the excellence of theology and the style of scripture. He even tried his hand at a Christian novel, *The Martyrdom of Theodora and Didymus*.

He died in London on 30 December 1691, and was buried in the Church of St Martin's-in-the-Fields, next to his dearest sister, Katherine, Lady Ranelagh. He never married.

Boyle was instrumental in establishing The Royal Society, the oldest continuing scientific society in the world. But despite his reputation, Dorset remained important to him. He described himself as 'Robert Boyle of Stalbridge' in his will, and endowed a school for 20 poor boys at Yetminster whose buildings still remain.

Benjamin Jesty (1737-1816), the first vaccinator

Benjamin Jesty was born in Yetminster and grew up to become a well-respected tenant farmer, living with his wife and family at Upbury farmhouse next to St Andrew's Church in the centre of the village.

The late eighteenth century was a revolutionary time for farming and an intelligent man like Jesty was perfectly suited to the age. He was prepared to embrace new ideas and thrived on the potential for prosperity. But he was also acquainted with the folklore of the farming community and knew that herdsmen and dairymaids who had caught cowpox never contracted the killer disease, smallpox.

In 1774, when he was 37 years old, there was a local outbreak of smallpox and Jesty was determined that his family would not be struck down with the disease. By then he had been married for four years to Elizabeth, and they had three children – two sons, Robert (3) and Benjamin (2), and a baby daughter, Elizabeth.

Jesty realised that he could deliberately infect his family with cowpox lymph and ensure their protection. Knowing that there was a herd of cows showing symptoms of cowpox in Chetnole, he and his wife and their two sons made their way on foot the few miles to the neighbouring village and there in a dairy field a historic event took place.

With a stocking needle he introduced material from lesions on the cows' udders into the arm of each of his family in turn, except baby Elizabeth, who was deemed too young. Jesty himself had been infected with cowpox as a young man, so he knew that he was already immune. He also knew that he was taking a calculated gamble with his family. Socially this took its toll, for he was ostracised and reviled by many of his neighbours who saw how ill his wife became, although afterwards she made a complete recovery. Many were acting out of ignorance, because there was still a widespread superstition that if you caught cowpox you might grow horns!

Many years later Jesty's two sons were inoculated with smallpox by a surgeon in Cerne Abbas. They did not develop its symptoms, thus proving the efficacy of his original vaccination.

In 1797 he and his family moved to Downshay Farm on the Isle of Purbeck. Benjamin and Elizabeth's final resting place is in the churchyard of St Nicholas of Myra at Worth Matravers, where their headstones stand side by side.

It was not until late in Jesty's life that the medical fraternity recognised him as the true originator of vaccination (from Latin *vacca*, a cow), rather than Edward Jenner (who performed his first inoculation in 1796). In the year of Trafalgar, 1805, his achievements were brought to light by Dr Andrew Bell, Rector of Swanage, who arranged a visit to London, where Jesty was invited to give evidence to the Original Vaccine Pock Institute. So impressed were the panel of doctors by the old farmer's pioneering spirit that they presented him with a pair of gold-mounted lancets, a testimonial scroll and fifteen guineas expenses. As a further token of respect they had his portrait painted by Michael William Sharp, a portraitist at the Royal Academy.

Mary Anning (1799-1847), pioneering palaeontologist

Remembered chiefly for her discovery in 1811 of the first complete *ichthyosaur* ever seen, Mary Anning lived her entire life in Lyme Regis. Her father, a carpenter, used to take Mary and her elder brother Joseph along the beach in search of fossils, which he sold at his shop as 'curiosities' to wealthy visitors to the newly fashionable resort.

Sadly, Mary's father died of consumption in 1810 when she was ten. An already impoverished childhood might have degenerated still further had it not been for the enterprise of the two youngsters. Well-versed in the skills needed for the collection of fossils, the two decided to carry on selling these curiosities from the shop. The patronage of such as Henry Henley, Lord of the nearby Manor of Colway, ensured that Mary and her brother did not actually starve.

It was another patron, a Lieutenant-Colonel Birch from Lincolnshire, who eventually put Mary on her feet. The Colonel was a regular visitor and frequently purchased fossils from the shop. He had noticed the poverty of the household and when she was twenty he sold his entire collection of fossils and gave the proceeds of £400 (a considerable sum of money in those days) to Mary, who thus became financially secure.

Her next major find was a perfect skeleton of a *plesiosaur* in 1824, which was bought by the Duke of Buckingham for £100. Four years later an even more astonishing find consisted of a *pterodactyl*, a gliding reptile whose remains are rare to this day. In 1832 she found another, larger *ichthyosaur* which now greets the visitor in the Natural History Museum in London.

She had a vast knowledge of her subject and her achievements were recognised by the Geological Society, who made her an honorary member as a tribute to the help that she had given to the many geologists who had visited her in Lyme Regis. She was known to be somewhat chagrined by the fact that they picked her brains and then went away and made money from their publications while she received nothing, but she enjoyed the intellectual stimulation that their visits entailed and she maintained a correspondence with a large number of geologists and fellow palaeontologists.

By nature she was probably a solitary person and a description of her, at the time of her second *ichthyosaur* discovery, does not give a very flattering picture, describing 'a prim, pedantic, vinegar-looking, thin female, shrewd and rather satirical in her conversation.' A portrait of her, with her spaniel at her feet and Lyme Bay in the background, painted by an unknown artist around 1840, gives a kinder impression, and is included in this book (the original can be seen at the Natural History Museum).

Indisputably she carved out for herself a formidable scientific reputation and The Royal Society honoured her by helping to fund the installation of a stained-glass window to her memory in Lyme Regis parish church.

John Gould (1804-1881), the British Audubon

John Gould, the 'British Audubon', was one of the most important and productive ornithological illustrators of the nineteenth century. During his lifetime he created over three thousand different hand-coloured lithographic plates of birds and animals, for clients that included both Queen Victoria and Prince Albert.

Gould was born in 1804 in Lyme Regis, the son of a gardener. He began to study birds and to learn taxidermy while assisting his father in the royal gardens at Windsor. By 1827, he was employed by the Zoological Society in the care of their ornithological collections, and in 1829 he published the first of nearly three hundred scientific articles.

In the same year he married Elizabeth Coxon, an accomplished artist who became his partner in the production of a long series of natural history monographs. These were distinguished for their fine colour plates, and were published serially or by subscription.

His most popular book was probably his monograph on hummingbirds, published between 1849 and 1861, but his greatest achievement was his monumental *Birds of Great Britain*, published between 1862 and 1873.

Together, John and Elizabeth Gould published seven major works, with 697 colour plates, over a period of fourteen years. Edward Lear assisted the Goulds during the production of two of these works and about 150 of the plates are his; the rest are the work of the Goulds.

Gould's wife died in 1841, and thereafter he employed other artists. He was an astute businessman, if severe in manner, who reputedly never knew his employees' Christian names. Nevertheless, he left his artists substantial bequests, and was willing, in his old age, with his life's work not yet completed, to spend time and effort to encourage young naturalists.

Over a period of fifty-seven years he published more than forty large folio volumes, the first set appearing in 1831, and the last in 1888, seven years after his death. Gould was, by his own confession, a self-made man, yet he left a priceless legacy of beauty and scientific knowledge. His series of natural history plates is considered by many to be the finest works of bird illustration ever presented.

Anthony Huxtable (1808-1883), pioneer of scientific farming

It has been said that society only becomes civilised when it learns how to manage its sewage. If this is the case, then Anthony Huxtable, a little-known Dorset parson, made an invaluable contribution to civilisation.

Born in 1808 in Somerset, son of a Bristol surgeon, Huxtable read Maths at Cambridge. Shortly after being ordained in 1834, he was offered the living at Sutton Waldron – midway between Blandford and Shaftesbury on the eastern rim of the Blackmore Vale – by Henry Sturt, the local landowner.

Huxtable found himself in a run-down community, where farming was backward. Without delay he set about an ambitious programme of improvement founded on scientific methods.

In 1840 he married Maria Langstone, who not only shared her husband's interests, but more importantly was willing to share her wealth – which was considerable. A new rectory was built, the derelict Saxon church demolished and replaced by the graceful edifice we see today. New cottages for farm-workers were constructed and a village school was established.

Huxtable was a tenant of two farms which he worked on scientific principles. Some of his experiments were years ahead of their time. One of these was the use of manure to grow swedes on barren land. He measured the ingredients under precise conditions, resulting in a magnificent yield of twenty-one tons to the acre, with a return of 300% on the outlay.

He studied various methods of feeding and sheltering stock, with much improved results, but his principal interest was the collection, storage and application of liquid manure. He built large tanks for the purpose and the manure was delivered to remote parts of fields through underground pipes. Solid manure was stored under cover, mixed with burnt clay, ash or sawdust. Steam power was used for threshing, pumping of manure, root-cutting and sack-filling, and the surplus heat from the engine was used to dry grain.

Huxtable pioneered the filtration of manure. He found that not only was the treated soil high in nutrients, and therefore invaluable as fertiliser, but the end product was clean water. This had enormous implications with regard to the treatment of sewage and avoidance of river pollution, and today's farmers and water boards owe a great deal to Huxtable's experiments.

In 1862, Huxtable became Archdeacon of Dorset, though sadly he had to retire from the post after only a few months owing to ill health. In 1874 he suffered a further blow when his wife of thirty-four years, Maria, died, but he rallied and re-married the following year. Gradually, Huxtable's health began to fail and he died in Sutton Waldron in 1883. His second wife, Susannah Gott, who survived him, set up a charity in his name for the relief of the local poor.

Alfred Russel Wallace (1823-1913), evolutionist, naturalist and social critic

Overshadowed by Charles Darwin, Alfred Russel Wallace is reckoned by some to be the true originator of the principle of natural selection, with the publication in 1855 of his 'Sarawak Law' essay, predating Darwin's 1858 writings.

While advancing the theory of organic *evolution*, Wallace's essay contains no hint of the notion of natural selection. Instead, he discusses the geological/geographical pattern of species divergence, referring to such divergences as 'creations', an indication that he had no grasp of the generating process, just its results.

Having laid to rest this particular misconception, there is little doubt that Wallace's work as a naturalist places him at the heart of a revolutionary change in thinking. His distinguished career ranks in many ways alongside that of Darwin's.

Wallace was born in Monmouthshire, initially training as a surveyor. A chance meeting with the naturalist Henry Bates awoke Wallace's own interest in natural history, and in 1848 the two men sailed for the Amazon for a collecting expedition that lasted four years.

He wrote up his expedition in *Palm Trees of the Amazon* and *A Narrative of Travels on the Amazon and Rio Negro*. He then set off again, this time for the Far East and for eight years, returning in 1862. This was a seminal period for Wallace, for while on Sarawak, he wrote *On the Tendency of Varieties to Depart Indefinitely from the Original Type* (1858), sending it off to Charles Darwin for comment, which resulted in his and Darwin's writings on natural selection being presented to the Linnaean Society.

In November 1859 Wallace's paper *On the Zoological Geography of the Malay Archipelago* was read before the Linnaean Society, giving the name 'Wallace Line' to the significant demarcation, which he observed, between the areas supporting Asian and Australasian faunas. In the same month, one of the greatest publishing events of all time occurred with the publication of Darwin's *The Origin of Species*.

The next 30 years saw Wallace marry, and the publication of a series of books and papers that gradually added to his reputation. In 1889 Wallace, aged 66, moved to Parkstone, and a further prolific period of writing ensued, combined with honours received for his services to natural history. In 1902, by now a Fellow of The Royal Society and one of the most distinguished scientists of the age, he moved to Old Orchard, Broadstone. Aside from his natural history, he was an outspoken advocate of socialism, pacifism and women's rights.

In 1908 his name was linked officially with Darwin when he received the Darwin-Wallace Medal of the Linnaean Society of London, and in December of the same year he received the Copley Medal from the Royal Society, and the Order of Merit from King Edward VII at Buckingham Palace.

Alfred Russel Wallace died peacefully at Old Orchard in November 1913 and was buried in Broadstone Cemetery, underneath a fossilised tree trunk, which stands proudly erect above his grave, a fitting memorial to this unusual and talented man.

In 2000, Wallace's restored grave was unveiled before a crowd, including three biographers, two grandsons, several great-grandchildren, and a great-great-grandson. Appropriately, a great-grandson of Darwin's was present. The local press report described the grave as having been 'handsomely restored, except for the fossilised tree trunk, which was declared to be in excellent condition after several hundred thousand years.'

Sir Frederick Treves (1853-1923), surgeon and author

The rise of Frederick Treves from son of Dorchester upholsterer and furniture maker to royal surgeon and a knighthood was remarkable. It began at the Dorchester school run by William Barnes, better known as Dorset's greatest dialect poet. Treves remembered Barnes as 'the gentlest and kindliest of men', adding that 'during school hours he was in the habit of pacing the room in a reverie, happily unconscious of his dull surroundings.'

From there he went to the Merchant Taylors' School in London, to University College, London, to study medicine, and then to the Medical School of the London Hospital. In 1884, aged thirty-one, Treves became full surgeon at the London Hospital. Later in the year he met Joseph Merrick, the 'Elephant Man', who became his 'greatest pathological success', despite Treves' inability to diagnose his condition. Treves ultimately rescued Merrick from destitution, creating a home for him in the attic of the London Hospital, until his death in 1890.

Treves is best known for his pioneering work in diseases of the appendix. He advocated operative treatment for appendicitis, and was the first to advise that, in chronic cases, operating should be delayed until a 'quiescent interval' had passed.

He served as consulting surgeon to the field forces in the Boer War and was present at the relief of Ladysmith. Upon his return to England in 1900 he was appointed Surgeon Extraordinary to Queen Victoria.

Two years later Treves' fame spread suddenly across the world when, in June 1902, two days before his coronation, King Edward VII became acutely ill with appendicitis. Treves operated on the King, who made a good recovery and was crowned in August. Treves became a baronet and his consulting room at No. 6 Wimpole Street 'one of the best known in England'. He was later made 'serjeant-surgeon' to King George V in 1910, as he had been to King Edward VII.

After his retirement from professional work in 1908, Treves helped found the British Red Cross Society. He also served as an examiner in anatomy and surgery for several years at the Royal College of Surgeons, and at the universities of Cambridge, Aberdeen and Durham. He received several honorary degrees, and was elected to the Rectorship of Aberdeen University, 1905-1908.

It has been said that Treves was 'a man of many-sided genius and widely varied achievement'. He was a successful travel writer, and his many publications include the much loved *Highways and Byways of Dorset*, published in 1906, still one of the most collectable books about the county. He was also, throughout his life, a keen athlete and an accomplished sailor, holding his Master Mariner's ticket.

During the First World War, Treves served at the War Office as President of the Headquarters Medical Board. In 1920, he moved first to the south of France, and then to Vevey, on Lake Geneva, where he died in December 1923, after a few days' illness. He died of peritonitis, ironically the disease in which he was the expert.

The great man's ashes were buried in Dorchester Cemetery, at a service arranged by his lifelong friend Thomas Hardy, who wrote a poem especially for the occasion. Treves had two daughters; the elder survived him; the younger had died, in 1900, of acute appendicitis. The Treves Surgical Unit at Dorchester Hospital is dedicated to his memory.

Sir Alfred Downing Fripp (1865-1930), Surgeon in Ordinary to Edward VII and King George V

Born in Blandford in 1865, Alfred Downing Fripp retained a close association with Dorset throughout his life. He loved the Dorset coast, spending many holidays there with his family. He eventually bought a property, the Mill House, in West Lulworth, in 1911, retiring there in 1925.

He was the son of the distinguished watercolourist, Alfred Downing Fripp, and his great-grandfather was the marine artist, Nicholas Pocock, whose depictions of sea battles such as Trafalgar, Cape St Vincent, Copenhagen and the Nile are rated amongst the finest in marine art.

Fripp, however, opted for the surgical knife not the palette knife, becoming Senior Surgeon at Guy's Hospital, where he lectured and wrote about the study of anatomy. From 1897-1910 he was Surgeon in Ordinary to King Edward VII, and from 1910 he held the same post for King George V.

In 1898, as Surgeon on board the Royal Yacht *Osborne*, Fripp was amongst the earliest users of Guglielmo Marconi's new system of wireless telegraphy, sending regular bulletins to Queen Victoria at

Osborne House on the progress of the Prince of Wales, who was convalescing on the Royal Yacht at Cowes after hurting his knee at a ball in Paris.

Fripp played an important role in the Boer War, serving as Senior Surgeon at the military hospital opened at Deelfontein in 1900. Ideally placed on a railway junction and 1,359 metres above sea level, with a bracing climate and a good water supply, the whole complex was a model example of a field hospital. This was due largely to Fripp who was so appalled at how things were run that he took it upon himself to ensure that the RAMC was reorganised, rendering it more effective, especially in wartime. For these services Fripp was rewarded with a knighthood in 1903, and he was created KCVO in 1906.

Back in London, Fripp's fame as a surgeon grew, and in September 1907, a dapper caricature of him by 'Spy', titled 'Master of the Knife', appeared in *Vanity Fair*.

Fripp was chairman of 'Ye Ancient Order of Froth Blowers', set up during the 1920s by himself and Mr Bert Temple, a wealthy patient and friend, to raise money for children's charities and hospitals. Very large sums of money were given to help the 'wee waifs' of London's East End.

When not in London, Fripp would join his family at the Mill House in Lulworth. In 1927 he had a second home built on the clifftop to its west, which he named 'Weston', in honour of his good friend, Sir George Holford, the developer of the famous arboretum at Westonbirt in Gloucestershire. Sir George had left Sir Alfred a handsome legacy and the latter wanted to repay his friend by constructing a fine house, designed by Sir Edwin Lutyens. At the back of the house rainwater drains from the roof into a superb water tank salvaged from Guy's Hospital, inscribed with the date 1770 and the hospital's name, serving as a constant reminder of a lifetime's work.

Sir Alfred Downing Fripp died at West Lulworth in 1930, aged 65, and is buried in the family plot at the Norman church of Holy Trinity in the village. Two years after his death a fellowship bearing his name was established at Guy's Hospital, a fitting tribute to an eminent surgeon who was also a warm-hearted family man.

Marie Stopes (1880-1958), advocate of birth control

'Jeanie, Jeanie, full of hopes,
Read a book by Marie Stopes.
Now, to judge by her condition,
She must have read the wrong edition.'

So runs a rhyme chanted by London schoolchildren in the 1920s, an indication of how famous Marie Stopes had become through her pioneering work in sex education and birth control.

Born in Edinburgh in 1880, Marie Stopes was the daughter of intellectual and enlightened parents. Her father was a distinguished scientist, and her feminist mother was the first woman in Scotland to obtain a university certificate. For a woman, this was no mean feat. Women were not allowed to attend lectures, nor were they permitted to be awarded a degree – hence the lowly certificate.

Aged eighteen, Stopes won a science scholarship at University College, London. She was a talented and committed student, and in 1901 achieved a double honours degree in botany and geology. Four years later she became Britain's youngest Doctor of Science.

Following in her mother's footsteps, Stopes supported the women's suffrage movement, eventually joining the Women's Freedom League.

Several unsuccessful love affairs were followed by an unlikely marriage in 1911 to Reginald Gates, who held traditional views of a woman's role in society. He strongly disapproved of her membership of the Women's Freedom League, and five years later the marriage was annulled for non-consummation.

At the same time, while the First World War was raging, Stopes began a book about feminism and marriage, *Married Love*. In it she argued that marriage should be an equal partnership between husband and wife: 'marriage', she wrote, 'can never reach its full stature until women possess as much intellectual freedom, and freedom of opportunity within it, as do their partners.'

This was such a revolutionary and controversial notion that no publisher would risk taking on the book. One stated that its theme was far ahead of its time and that publication should wait 'until after the war.' Since no one knew when the war would end, this was tantamount to a rejection. Stopes persevered, and *Married Love* was finally published in March 1918. The book was an immediate success, selling 2,000 copies within a fortnight. By the end of the year it had reprinted six times. It gave rise to a flood of correspondence from ordinary women who yearned for more freedom, and more understanding from their husbands, as well as causing a storm in the establishment. In America, the book was declared obscene and quickly banned.

Her next book, *Wise Parenthood*, was equally controversial. It was a concise guide to contraception, based on the observation that many women died of self-induced abortions, or raised large families in poverty. It created yet another storm, invoking the wrath of the Church of England, which believed that it was wrong to advocate the use of birth control, and the Roman Catholic Church, which condemned all forms of contraception.

Undeterred, Stopes continued her campaign, and in 1921 founded the Society for Constructive Birth Control, with financial help from her wealthy second husband, the aviator Humphrey Roe, who enthusiastically supported her views. In March the same year she also opened the first of her birth-control clinics in Holloway, North London.

Stopes campaigned tirelessly on other fronts as well, such as attempting to stop education authorities from sacking women teachers when they got married, and persuading the Inland Revenue to allow husbands and wives to be taxed separately. These are liberties we take for granted. *Wise Parenthood* and *Married Love* now seem totally innocuous, but, at the time, a crusade such as Stopes' risked prosecution and imprisonment.

In spite of her stance on marriage, Stopes' own marriage to Humphrey Roe was not a model relationship. Though they had loved each other dearly in the early years, Stopes became so busy and famous that she had a tendency to appear aloof, even arrogant and vain, and Roe felt keenly that he was in his wife's shadow.

Nevertheless, they bought a romantic holiday home on the Isle of Portland as a retreat from her fame, and it was there that their first and only child, Harry, was conceived, her pregnancy giving rise to the playground poem with which I began this piece. The property was Upper Light, the old lighthouse on Portland Bill, sold off as redundant by Trinity House in 1906. This was to be her home for many years.

Marie Stopes was a great benefactor to Portland. She gave the Island a pair of cottages at Wakeham, which after being converted opened in 1922 as Portland Museum, and today remain the home for many treasures connected to the Island's long history.

Roe died in 1949, aged seventy. Dr Stopes, for her part, believed she was indestructible. She swam in the heavy seas off Portland Bill, stating that she would not feel middle-aged until she was a hundred.

In her will, she wrote, with characteristic vigour, 'I most emphatically wish to be cremated – at Golders Green, and to have my ashes scattered on the sea as near the Race as a fisherman can safely go, at Portland Bill, Dorset.'

She died in 1958, a few days before her seventy-eighth birthday, and her son did his best to respect her wishes. All Dorset fishermen know the perils of sailing close to the Portland Race. Not wishing to endanger life in pursuit of his mother's request, Harry mounted a high rock, and scattered her ashes into the sea off Portland Bill.

One of Marie Stopes' ambitions had been to see the State accept responsibility for the provision of birth control services. Had she lived to the 'middle-age' she was expecting, she would have seen, in 1975, a law passed that gives every woman in Britain the right to free contraception.

Professor Michael House (1930-2002), geologist who specialised in the fossil wealth of the South-West

Born in Blandford Forum in 1930, Michael Robert House was the son of a Portland dockyard master plumber. He went to school in Weymouth, and after National Service studied at Cambridge, where he was greatly influenced by the specialist in Jurassic studies W. J. Arkell, who persuaded him that rather than follow his own instincts and study Jurassic ammonites, he should study their poorly known ancestors in the earlier Devonian rocks.

Such was his promise at Cambridge that by the time of his graduation in 1954, he had been appointed to a lectureship in geology at Durham, where the head of the department, K.C. (later Sir Kingsley) Dunham provided an inspirational model for his academic life.

While at Durham, House set about finding ammonoids in the highly deformed rocks of south-west England, and using them, together with the toothed conodont microfossils, as tools in dating the Devonian rocks and elucidating their structure.

In 1963 House left Durham for a lectureship at Oxford, but by 1967 his reputation ensured him the Chair of Geology at Hull. He was Dean of Science from 1976-78 and Pro-Vice-Chancellor from 1980-83.

The wider geological community knew him through his presidencies of the Yorkshire Geological Society, the Palaeontological Association, the Palaeontological Society and the Systematics Association.

House's awards were many, and include the Murchison Medal of the Geological Society, presented in 1991. He produced an impressive array of more than 150 publications, and his classic guide to the geology of the Dorset coast has provided the mainstay for many amateur as well as professional geologists.

In retirement in Weymouth he enjoyed the company of local enthusiasts in the field and continued his active research. His death in 2002 left a huge gap in geological circles, locally, nationally and internationally.

To the general public Professor Michael House will be remembered for his significant contribution to the successful bid for UNESCO World Heritage status for the East Devon and Dorset coasts.

SEVEN

Shining Lights

Saint Judith (circa 7th century), Saint's Day 13 July

Saint Judith's dates are uncertain, but not so the bizarre events that led to her martyrdom.

She lived in Halstock, whose name derives from Halgan Stone, or Holy Place, and whose religious community had become an important place of pilgrimage.

Judith was famed both for her piety and hospitality. She regularly welcomed pilgrims into her home, and when her mother died she and her brother, Bana, and her sisters, Sidwella, Wilgitha and Edwara (later to become Cornish saints), continued to live in their father's home. Her troubles began with her father's remarriage. The new step-mother quickly became jealous of her pious step-daughter and secretly began to hatch plans to get rid of her.

Judith spent long hours fasting and kneeling in devotion. When she started to complain of chest pains, the step-mother saw her chance. Pretending to be of help, she suggested that if Judith applied a freshly-made cheese to her chest, the pain would be relieved. Judith did as instructed, not minding the milky deposits left on the front of her undergarments. Meanwhile, the step-mother went to Bana, claiming that Judith was pregnant. Bana flew into a rage and confronted Judith, who meekly denied the accusation. Her brother ordered her to remove her dress. Seeing the soiled undergarments, he took this as evidence of her guilt, drew his sword and smote off her head.

Folklore has embellished the narrative from this point, for Judith is reputed to have picked up her head and carried it to the church, placing it on the altar as a plea to God to recognise her innocence.

The community soon realised that Judith had been unjustly condemned. The step-mother was shunned, and Judith's father banished her from his home. Judith was given a Christian burial in the

91

churchyard at Halstock, and in the tenth century her remains were disinterred and transferred to St Wulfstan's Church in Sherborne, where many miracles are said to have taken place at her tomb.

The place of her death, Abbot's Hill in Halstock, is popularly known as Judith's Hill, and nearby is Chapel Close, where the Priory was built, probably on the site of her home. The village pub, The Quiet Woman, continues to be a reminder of Judith's martyrdom, with its inn-sign depicting Saint Judith carrying her head.

Saint Aldhelm (639-709),
first Bishop of Sherborne, Saint's Day 25 May

Scholar, evangelist, poet and musician, Saint Aldhelm was appointed the first Bishop of Sherborne in 705, making 2005 the thirteen hundredth anniversary of the founding of Sherborne Abbey.

This occurred when the Bishopric of Wessex was split into two dioceses by King Ine. Aldhelm only reluctantly agreed to accept the appointment. Then aged sixty-six, he knew that the onerous duties of such a post might shorten his life and give him less time to devote to his studies. His fears were justified, as he only lived another four years.

During that time he left an indelible mark on Dorset. The stone chapel on the windswept promontory of St Aldhelm's Head almost certainly replaced a Saxon original, and the chapel's name may point to Aldhelm being its founder. He certainly established the Nunnery of Saint Mary at Wareham, built churches at Langton Matravers and the royal palace of Corfe, and, most importantly of all, he set to work rebuilding a church in Sherborne, some of whose stonework still remains. Indisputably it is to Aldhelm that we owe, albeit indirectly, the glorious example of Perpendicular architecture that can be seen today.

But what of the man? Aldhelm was born in Wessex in 639, and was probably related to King Ine. While still a boy, he was sent to Canterbury to be educated. After returning to Wessex, he joined the scholastic community at Malmesbury. As his reputation spread, the community was joined by scholars from France and Scotland. Aldhelm is said to have been able to write and speak Latin and Greek, and to have been able to read the Old Testament in Hebrew. The voluntary association of this gathering of scholars changed its status around 683 when they were formed into a regular Benedictine monastery, with

Aldhelm as their Abbot. Under his leadership the Abbey of Malmesbury grew to be a renowned seat of piety and learning, and it is significant that when he was appointed Bishop of Sherborne he was allowed to retain the Abbacy of Malmesbury, no doubt in honour of his long-standing influence there.

Aldhelm was not a voluminous writer, but the two treatises that have given celebrity to his name (*In Praise of Virginity* and his *Aenigmata*) stand proud in the annals of early English scholarship. It has been said that 'Aldhelm was the first Englishman who cultivated classical learning with any success, and the first of whom any literary remains are preserved.' He also wrote in Anglo-Saxon, which led King Alfred the Great to place him in the first rank of the vernacular poets. As late as the twelfth century, some ballads he had composed continued to be popular.

To be a poet, in those days, you also had to be a musician, and it appears that Aldhelm excelled on all the different instruments then in use, including the harp, fiddle and pipes. Long after he became Abbot of Malmesbury, Aldhelm devoted much of his leisure time to music and poetry, though he was also known for his austerity. It is particularly recorded of him that he was wont to recite the entire Psalter standing up to his neck in ice-cold water.

Aldhelm died at Doulting in Somerset in 709, and his body was conveyed to Malmesbury, a distance of fifty miles. Crosses were erected every seven miles along the way at each halting place where his remains rested for the night, and it was not long before his body was placed in a magnificent shrine and revered as a saint.

Saint Walburga (circa 710-779), Saint's Day 1 May
Though born in Devon and spending much of her life in Germany, Walburga established a lasting connection with Dorset by living in the county for twenty-seven years.

She came from a deeply religious background. Her two brothers, Winnibald and Willibald, later became saints. Her uncle was to become the celebrated Saint Boniface. A cousin, Lioba, was already a nun at Wimborne when Walburga joined her and took vows at an early age.

During Walburga's long residence at Wimborne, her brothers accompanied Boniface as missionaries to Northern Europe to convert the heathen in an area corresponding roughly to present-day Germany. Boniface wrote to the Abbess Tetta of Wimborne asking for a group of nuns to go out and help them in their task, amongst whom was Walburga.

Walburga's brothers had by then founded a monastery at Heidenheim, and Walburga became Abbess in charge of the nuns attached to it. Later she became Abbess of the whole monastery, monks as well as nuns. She had a wide knowledge of medicine and understood herbal remedies and natural cures. These had been learned during her time at Wimborne amongst the rich flora of Dorset, and she is usually depicted carrying an ampulla of healing oil.

Walburga died in 779. A century later her bones were moved and reburied beside her brother. When her bones were disinterred, it was noticed that an oily substance was dripping from them, which was found to have healing properties. Over the centuries the oil continued to flow and was collected regularly by the nuns, who bottled it in tiny phials and sent it all over the world to effect cures.

Accordingly, Walburga has become one of the best known saints, but she has a strange, pagan connection, because of the Church's selection of May Day as her Saints' Day, a traditional day of celebration and probably chosen in an attempt to suppress the rituals of May Day Eve (known as Beltane), when witches appeared riding broomsticks or he-goats, and consorted with the Devil. The plan backfired and the pagan superstitions continued as before, only the name Beltane fell out of use and was changed to Walburga's Night, or, as it is still known in Germany, 'Walpurgisnacht'.

Legend has it that Saint Walburga's protection gives complete security against all evil spells.

John White (1575-1648), Patriarch of Dorchester

Every Sunday worshippers at St Peter's Church, Dorchester, step over a Dorset worthy, John White, for it is in the porch of this church that his tomb lies.

White was a man of many parts – a talented scholar, a powerful preacher (he preached to the Long Parliament of Oliver Cromwell), a charitable benefactor (he was deeply involved in the organisation of a public subscription to establish a hospital in Dorchester), a notable headmaster (he was headmaster of Hardye's School from 1632 to

1635) and a founding father of the Massachusetts Bay Colony in the USA.

White played a crucial role in encouraging the Dorset emigrants who sailed in the *Mary and John* in 1630, preaching to them on board ship before they set sail. One of the groups he sent out founded the American town of Dorchester, and the first church they built was called the 'Daughter of John White'. It is still known as that to this day, thus confirming the words of his epitaph in St Peter's porch, 'his name lives in unfading remembrance.'

Throughout that troubled time of savage repression of Catholicism and the ascendancy of Protestantism, White presided over the Puritan spirit of Dorchester. The reverence in which he was held was almost iconic. One contemporary described him as 'a man who stains all other men's lives with the clearness of his own.' His epitaph in St Peter's describes him as 'a man of great godliness, good scholarship and a wonderful ability and kindness.' The townspeople were more to the point, dubbing him 'Patriarch of Dorchester'.

William Wake (1657-1736), Archbishop of Canterbury

William Wake was a descendant of his legendary namesake, Hereward, and was, by all accounts, of equally determined character.

Wake was born in the village of Shapwick in 1657, and quickly made his mark as a brilliant scholar, first of all in Blandford, and then by matriculating at Oxford at the tender age of sixteen.

In 1682 he was ordained, initially serving as a chaplain at the Court of Louis XIV. Seven years later, aged 32 and newly married (his long-suffering wife Ethelreda bore him thirteen children), he was appointed Canon of Christchurch College, Oxford, and made Rector of St James, Westminster.

Such a meteoric rise seemed to indicate that Wake was destined for even greater things to come. At a time of great political unrest his Protestantism put him on the side of the ascendant power, and following the accession of William and Mary, he was installed as Resident Canon of Exeter Cathedral in 1701. Next he became Bishop of Lincoln, soon afterwards being appointed to one of those arcane cathedral posts only to be found in the Church of England, namely 'Clerk of the Closet'. He was finally made Archbishop of Canterbury in 1715.

Archbishop Wake never forgot his Dorset origins, and one of the high spots of his life was to preach to the Society of Dorset Men in St Mary le Bow, when they met in London in 1690. He frequently returned home to Shapwick, and he took great pleasure in preaching in one of Dorset's gems, the twelfth century Church of St Andrew at Winterborne Tomson.

Wake believed that all children should have an equal chance of a good education, and he founded the Blue Coat School in Blandford. Strict rules ensured that its 'twelve poor boys' adhered to the Protestant religion and that they were trained to play their part in the trades and industry of Blandford. The charitable trust was wound up in 1974, but his name lives on in the new Blandford Primary School, which was dedicated by the Bishop of Sherborne and was renamed 'Archbishop Wake Junior School'.

John (1687-1770) and William (1689-1766) Bastard, brothers responsible for the rebuilding of Blandford

At the time of the devastating Blandford fire of 1731, John and William Bastard were in business in the town as architects, builders and joiners. They enjoyed a good reputation, having learned their trade from their father, Thomas, who had built Charlton Marshall church and the rectory at Spetisbury.

With their elder brother Thomas, they were the natural choice of the Trustees to undertake the planning and rebuilding of the town, and immediately set about compiling a detailed, priced inventory of the total losses. Before the work could begin, Thomas died, probably from the smallpox epidemic then raging in the town, leaving John and William to carry on.

The impact of the fire on Blandford was enormous. The inferno destroyed the parish church, the grammar school, the Town Hall and all but a dozen of the town's houses, public buildings, inns and business premises. The fire received wide publicity, and many cities, towns and individuals subscribed to an appeal for funds, including King George II (£1,000), Queen Caroline (£200), the Prince of Wales (£100), and William Wake, the Dorset-born Archbishop of Canterbury (see page 95) who had gone to school in Blandford (£100).

The Market Square was cleared of obstructions, including the old Town Hall, the Shambles and four cottages known as Middle Row,

96

Saint Aldhelm, first Bishop of Sherborne, founded Sherborne Abbey 1,300 years ago.
In celebration of this 2005 anniversary, a bronze sculpture of the saint was
commissioned from Italian-born Marzia Colonna, now living in Dorset. Dedicated in
July 2005 by the Bishop of Sherborne, the statue, seen here in choir of the abbey, is
now situated in the niche above the south porch (see page 92).

Marjorie Winzar (left) stands by the joint headstone of her great-great-great-aunt Ann Winzer, nurse at Waterloo, and James Winzer, her soldier husband. The memorial in Piddlehinton churchyard was re-cut in 2001 by Ed Hall and re-dedicated in August 2002 by the Right Revd John Kirkham (retired Bishop of Sherborne). Marjorie is accompanied by two members of the Napoleonic Society who were dressed as Ann and James Winzer for the occasion (see page 98).

BELOW The Reverend Henry Deane, was vicar of Gillingham for half a century. The results of his labours remain visible throughout North Dorset (see page 99).

BELOW Thomas Hollis of Corscombe, 18th century philanthropist, Republican, and self-styled 'Citizen of the World' (see page 97).

ABOVE The 7th Earl of Shaftesbury, Anthony Ashley-Cooper, seen here at St Giles House, Wimborne St Giles, with his wife Minny, was a prime mover of social reform in the mid-19th century. He did much to improve the lot of industrial and factory workers, especially children who were often mercilessly exploited (see page 101).

RIGHT The Reverend Lord Sidney Godolphin Osborne, vicar of Durweston between 1841 and 1875, campaigned on behalf of Dorset's agricultural labourers (see page 102).

Lady Charlotte Guest , mother-in-law of Cornelia, 1st Lady Wimborne.

Mother and daughter-in-law spanned 77 years of occupation of Canford House and its vast estate, showering benefits on the local community, including the building of three schools and 108 model cottages.

Lady Charlotte's son, Ivor, married Cornelia Spencer-Churchill, daughter of the Duke of Marlborough. Ivor was created Lord Wimborne in 1880, and Lady Wimborne went on to found the Cornelia Hospital, now the site of Poole General Hospital. Her name lives on in the Cornelia Nurses Home nearby (see pages 103 & 108).

General-Pitt Rivers, 'Father of British Archaeology', set standards for recording archaeological finds on which modern methods are still based. His fine collections were once displayed at the Farnham Museum, near Tollard Royal, but are now in the British Museum or at the Pitt-Rivers Museum in Oxford (see page 105).

On Whit Monday 1893 Daniel
(later Sir Dan) Godfrey signed a
contract with the Mayor of
Bournemouth to found a town
band, and thus began the renowned
Bournemouth Municipal Orchestra,
later to become the world-famous
Bournemouth Symphony Orchestra
(see page 110).

Inspector Frederick Abbeline was the
officer in charge of the Jack the Ripper
case, which shook London in the late
1880s. The case was never solved and
echoes down to this day (see page 106).

Lord Baden-Powell founded the Boy Scout Movement with the first Scout Camp on Brownsea Island in 1907. The photograph above shows the camp, which consisted of 22 boys from different social backgrounds. The Union Jack flew from a cavalry lance and was the flag that had flown over his headquarters at Mafeking during the Boer War.

The photograph on the left shows Baden-Powell on Brownsea Island during the first camp.

The Movement now numbers over 400 million members in countries all over the world (see page 109).

Alan Cobham about to land on the Thames beside the Houses of Parliament in 1926 in an attempt to publicise civil aviation and passenger-carrying flights. Cobham was later knighted. His principal legacy is air-to-air refuelling, which he experimented with from Tarrant Rushton Aerodrome, setting world records for in-flight refuelling (see page 112).

ABOVE LEFT Rolf Gardiner of Springhead, Fontmell Magna, championed organic farming and was a founder member of the Soil Association. He gave prophetic warnings about misuse of the environment (see page 114).

ABOVE RIGHT For many Ralph Wightman was the voice of radio in the 1930s, 40s and 50s. His rich Dorset dialect charmed all those who heard him and he became a national celebrity. His voice was likened to 'heather honey, goose grease and just plain comic.' (see page 113).

BELOW Artist Simon Combes was passionate about wildlife. He sat on boards of several conservation organisations and raised, through his art, large sums of money for their causes. Tragically he was killed by a buffalo in Kenya in 2004 (see page 115).

thereby creating an early example of town planning.

One of their principal projects was the church, which was started in 1735. The cupola was never part of the original design, which had a spire, and one of the brothers' enduring disappointments was that the cupola was substituted for financial reasons. They referred to it as 'a short lived wooden top', but it is still there.

The brothers celebrated the completion of their work in the Market Square in 1760 by erecting a pump, near the south-west angle of the churchyard, made of Portland stone. The original inscription, which is still located at the fountain, acknowledges Divine Mercy for raising 'this town, like the phoenix from its ashes, to its present beautiful and flourishing state.'

Blandford has not been visited by any such calamity since, and it seems that the Bastard family did well out of the rebuilding, becoming gentlemen of means with their own armorial bearings. One thing is certain – John and William Bastard, and those who worked under them – produced perhaps the most perfect example of a small Georgian country town anywhere in the British Isles.

Thomas Hollis (1720-1774), philanthropist and lover of liberty
Thomas Hollis was first and foremost a scholar and benefactor of Harvard University, the connection beginning with his uncle, who had given books and endowments to its library.

After a successful London-based career, Hollis retired to Urles Farm in Corscombe, to enjoy his 3,000 acre estate. There he rebuilt the church and set about naming his farms and fields according to his Whig and Republican sentiments.

To this day, Harvard Farm has fields named New England, Boston, Massachusetts, Adams, Revolution, William III, Settlement and Hanover. He named one wood Stuart, so that he could derive anti-Jacobite satisfaction by beheading it every time he coppiced or thinned its trees.

Locke Farm, Halstock, was named in tribute to the English philosopher, John Locke. Three of its fields were called Reasonableness, Comprehension and Understanding, drawn from Locke's works, and one was named Secker, after the then Archbishop, whom Hollis derided – the field in question was barren ground.

Liberty Farm predates the American War of Independence, but its name rings out in the spirit of the newly fledging nation.

Ascetic in all things, Hollis' diet excluded sugar, salt and spices, and he drank only water. He had a special affection for Urles Farm, describing it as 'a most healthy, and, I think, beautiful spot.' Of the soil he said 'the very earth itself is sweet beyond a nosegay.'

This energetic, self-styled 'Assertor of Liberty, Citizen of the World' died quite suddenly in 1774 whilst giving instructions to his farm workers. Hollis had ordered that his 'corpse be deposited in a grave ten feet deep, and that the field should be immediately ploughed over, that no trace of the burial-place might remain.' His last wishes were carried out to the letter and no one knows the exact location of this philanthropic man's remains.

Ann Winzer (1791-1873), Waterloo heroine

This remarkable lady, daughter of Joseph and Elizabeth Keats, was born in Fordington, where twenty years later in 1811 she married James Winzer. The alliance was to prove a momentous one, for James, a plasterer-journeyman by trade, enlisted in the army and found himself called to action by the Duke of Wellington, to fight Napoleon at the Battle of Waterloo.

Ann stayed loyally by her husband's side, and her story continues as told on her gravestone in Piddlehinton Churchyard: 'She was a Waterloo heroine who assisted at that famous battle A.D.1815 by aiding and assisting the sick and wounded.

'She endured many hardships, having followed the British Army from Brussels to Paris. From Paris to Duney [she] returned to England & from thence to the Rock of Gibraltar, where she remained 4 years.

'She afterwards resided in this Parish, where she received a pension through the instrumentality of Colonel Astell with that of many other officers, by whose kindness this stone is raised as a tribute of respect to a long life spent in true and faithful service.'

Ann Winzer died in 1873, aged 82, and James Winzer ended his days as a Chelsea Pensioner, dying just two years later, aged 85. Their epitaphs stands side by side, carefully engraved on twin headstones, surmounted by a simple cross.

Their story endures because the Colonel (later General) Astell mentioned on her gravestone lived in Piddlehinton and happened to be a Staff Officer on the Board of Pensioners, so would have had an intimate knowledge of Winzer's service record.

By the year 2000 the headstones had fallen into a state of illegible disrepair, and an appeal was launched by Geoff Lord to raise the funds necessary to renovate the memorial. Many people contributed to the appeal, both locally and from further afield, and a service of re-dedication was held in 2002 by the Right Reverend John Kirkham, retired Bishop of Sherborne. A member of the Napoleonic Society dressed for the occasion as a redcoat, another as Ann Winzer, and the Royal British Legion carried their colours.

Sadly, Lord died before the work was completed, but any visitor to Piddlehinton Churchyard can see the excellent repair work done by Ed Hall, who worked on site to re-script the text on the monuments, and who installed a slate plaque, at his own expense, recording Lord's connection with the fund.

Henry Deane (1799-1882), church builder and founder of schools

If the success of the Victorian era can be judged by the amount of church building that took place, then Henry Deane was undoubtedly a man of his times.

Appointed in 1832 as rector of Gillingham, Deane soon gave notice of his intentions. Finding that the only elementary school available to poor children was a recently established Infants' School, he promptly started a boys' evening school and a men's reading group. At Enmore Green he converted a cottage into a day school, using it also for Sunday evening services until he was able to build the beautiful little church he eventually placed there.

Deane's reconstructions and alterations began in earnest in 1837 (the year of his promotion to Rural Dean of Shaftesbury), when he lengthened Bourton Church, widened the chancel and built a side chapel for use as a Sunday school.

He next turned his attention to Gillingham church, arguing that the town's population of nearly 3,000 deserved better than the limited 200 free sittings of which fewer than 100 were 'within sight and hearing of the reading desk and pulpit.' His representations led to the complete rebuilding of St Mary's, with the exception of the chancel, at a cost of just over £3,000. Deane himself gave £550, and further contributions came from wealthy local families such as the Grosvenors.

In 1842 Deane was made a Prebendary of Salisbury Cathedral, but the following year his eldest daughter contracted scarlet fever and died, two months short of her ninth birthday. Deane and his wife immersed themselves in parish affairs, and continued their good works.

Already Deane had rebuilt the tower and nave of West Stour church (happily sparing the thirteenth century chancel, rather than pulling down the whole church, as originally proposed). East Stour church, also medieval, was not so fortunate – the church was completely demolished in 1841 and a new pseudo-Norman church built in its place.

In 1846 St Mary's Motcombe was reconstructed. Then Deane was struck by another personal tragedy, when his wife, Jane, died after a short illness. Once again he rose above his misfortunes, remarrying two years later.

His crowning achievement, architecturally speaking, was his final project at Milton. In 1867 a brand new church, St Simon and St Jude, was completed on a site donated by Thomas Matthews, owner of Matthews Brewery in Wyke. Matthews' family members gave substantial sums towards its construction, and it remains a gem of Victorian church architecture in 13th century style.

He continued to pursue his interest in education. Having established a little school at East Stour many years before, he replaced it with a new one in 1871, as well as starting another in West Stour, both of them serving the children of those parishes for the next fifty-five years.

His final educational work was the establishment of a Grammar School in Gillingham, which was formed in 1876 from the original Free School. The first chairman of the Board of Governors was none other than Henry Deane.

Few men of the cloth have made as much of their incumbency as did Henry Deane, albeit granted the unusually long span of fifty years in the same parish. The results of his works are all around, and North Dorset owes a great debt to this generous man, who combined vision with action.

Anthony Ashley-Cooper (1801-1885), 7th Earl of Shaftesbury, social reformer

In the early nineteenth century much of the working population worked long hours, in miserable conditions, poorly fed, badly lit and freezing cold. A significant part of that workforce consisted of children, routinely as young as seven. Many of the coal mines then being opened to help fuel the Industrial Revolution employed five-year olds. In one case, a child of three was found to be working as a 'trapper' (operating a string to open and close one of a series of ventilation doors in the mineshafts as the coal wagons passed through).

A leading light in the abolition of these malpractices was the Honourable Anthony Ashley-Cooper. Born in 1801 at Wimborne St Giles, he received a privileged education at Harrow and Oxford, entering public life in 1826 as MP for Woodstock, the pocket borough of his uncle, the Duke of Marlborough.

The turning point for Ashley-Cooper came when he was appointed a member of a Commission dealing with lunacy. Visiting asylums, he grew appalled at the dirt and squalor, and the wretched state of the inmates. There and then he determined to devote the rest of his life to the alleviation of suffering through legislation. His first step was the Ten Hours Bill, which sought to limit working hours to a maximum of ten hours for all between the ages of 9 and 18, and to prohibit the employment of children under the age of nine.

Encountering stiff opposition, Ashley-Cooper overcame personal shyness to speak forcefully in the Commons, and the 1833 Factory Act was passed, although it did not win him his ten-hour day. Nine years later, the 1842 Mines Act came into force, banning the underground employment of all women, and of children under ten, but Ashley-Cooper was bitterly disappointed by the reluctance of members of his own class to support much-needed social reform.

In 1851 he inherited the family estate at Wimborne St Giles, becoming the 7th Earl of Shaftesbury. To fund improvements, and to build new cottages and schools, he sold pictures and plate from the house, as well as a portion of the estate.

Returning to Parliament, Ashley-Cooper turned his attention to chimney sweeps. Young boys had to climb hot flues, which often caused severe burns, inhalation of soot, or even suffocation from smoke. In some cases their masters were rubbing the boys' elbows in strong solutions of brine to harden their flesh. Few ever washed, they were covered with vermin and frequently died of testicular cancer.

The relevant Act, prohibiting boys under the age of sixteen from working as sweeps, was not passed until 1875, but, in the meantime, the Earl had focused on the issue of child labour in the brickyards, where boys and girls struggled, half naked, carrying hods of wet clay, and suffering intense changes of temperature as they went to and fro from the hot kilns into the cold open air. Finally, a Bill was passed prohibiting women under sixteen, and all children under ten from working in the brickyards.

In 1882 the Earl's health began to fail, and he died three years later. A state funeral was held in Westminster Abbey, though the family insisted that the 7th Earl should be buried not in the Abbey, but in the churchyard in his beloved corner of Dorset, at Wimborne St Giles. His most enduring memorial is the legislation he helped push through Parliament, but his most visible is the statue of Eros in the middle of Piccadilly Circus, which was set up to commemorate all he had achieved, and whose bow and arrow were deliberately aligned on Wimborne St Giles.

Sidney Godolphin Osborne (1808-1889), champion of the rural poor
It might seem unlikely that a titled gentleman would be the incumbent of a small rural parish, such as Durweston near Blandford. Even more unlikely that he might also be an advocate for down-trodden farm workers, but both apply to The Honourable and Reverend Lord Sidney Godolphin Osborne, third son of the first Baron Godolphin.

Osborne's connection with Dorset began in 1841 when he was invited by Lord Portman of Bryanston House to take the Durweston living, remaining there for the next thirty-four years.

He quickly became aware of the high levels of local unemployment, and the squalid living conditions of the agricultural labourers in his own and neighbouring parishes. Together with his fellow clergy in nearby Stourpaine, he submitted evidence, couched in scathing criticism, to the Poor Law Commissioners, who published a report in 1843 regarding the exploitation of women and children in agriculture.

This did not go down well with the local landowners, and he soon gained a reputation for not mincing his words, nor being afraid to act on behalf of his disadvantaged parishioners.

He would frequently write hard-hitting letters to *The Times*, always signing himself 'S.G.O.', as he became popularly known. Osborne did not confine his efforts to campaigning in the press; he also believed that the Church should take some responsibility for the plight of the poor, and he urged his ecclesiastical superiors to take a stand on their behalf. He also wrote on Free Trade, Women's Rights, Sanitation, and Opportunities in the Colonies. Like John White of Dorchester two hundred years earlier, he encouraged young men and women to escape the misery of their lives by emigrating, not to America, but to Australia and Canada.

He campaigned vigorously for better administration, both in Ireland, after the famine, and later, in the Crimea. There he rolled up his sleeves and actually assisted in the military hospitals, where Florence Nightingale, too, was campaigning for better conditions.

The writer Charles Kingsley, author of *The Water Babies*, was married to Osborne's sister-in-law, Fanny, and was briefly curate of Pimperne, just three miles away over the hill. He and Fanny used to walk over to Durweston, and there can be no doubt that Kingsley's interest in social reform was influenced by Sidney Osborne.

Osborne's wife, Emily, died in 1875, and was buried at Durweston, as were three of their children. Osborne retired from his living that year, and moved to Lewes, Sussex, where he died in 1889, aged 81.

The Reverend Lord Sidney Godolphin Osborne was buried in the Churchyard of St John sub Castro in Lewes, but this forgotten hero was remarkable for his long connection with Dorset and for the huge efforts he made throughout his long life to improve the lot of the rural poor.

Lady Charlotte Guest (1812-1895), industrialist and scholar

Of the many women associated with Canford Manor over its long history, perhaps Lady Charlotte Guest's story is the most extraordinary, since she packed into her life more than most people do in several lifetimes.

In the course of her eighty-three years, she ran the largest ironworks in Great Britain; she was courted by Benjamin Disraeli; she collected fine porcelain (donated towards the end of her life to the Victoria and

Albert Museum); she translated the Welsh epic poem *The Mabinogion* into English (having taken the trouble to learn the language on her visits to the ironworks); and she knitted mufflers for London 'cabbies'.

Born Lady Charlotte Bertie, in 1812, she was the only daughter of the 9th Earl of Lindsey, and she came to live at Canford in 1846 as Lady Charlotte Guest, wife of Sir John Guest, owner of the immensely profitable Dowlais Iron Works, near Merthyr Tydfil.

Her childhood was unhappy. Her father died when she was six and her mother's second marriage was to a heavy drinker with a violent temper. Her saving grace came in a strange form. She had two mentally retarded brothers who required a private tutor, from whom she learned French, Italian, Latin, Greek, Hebrew and Persian. He also encouraged her musical aptitude on the piano and harp.

Her marriage to one of the richest industrialists in Britain enabled her to indulge her taste for improvements to Canford Manor. The house had been bought for the colossal sum of £335,000 and Lady Charlotte's transformation of it by Sir Charles Barry into a Gothic mansion cost a further £30,000.

It was her husband's declining health that had led to the choice of a house on the south coast (at the time he was sixty-one and she was only thirty-four). As his health deteriorated even further, she played an ever greater part in his affairs, taking complete control after his death in 1852 of a business on whom 12,000 families were dependent for their livelihood. The railway network in Britain was then expanding rapidly. Lady Charlotte saw its potential. She turned over the Dowlais Iron Works to the exclusive manufacture of railway lines, eventually supplying not only the domestic market but also Russia, the United States, and much of the Empire.

She had travelled abroad frequently with her husband, dividing her time between visiting iron works and factories with art galleries and museums. Astonishingly, she was also producing babies at a rate of roughly one a year until she had ten children, five boys and five girls over a period of twelve years! The eldest of these, Ivor, ultimately took over the running of the Dowlais Iron Works and the occupation of Canford Manor. This enabled Lady Charlotte to devote herself to her new husband, Charles Schreiber, who was thirteen years her junior, much to the disapproval of her children.

No longer encumbered with the management of the iron works,

Lady Charlotte began collecting seventeenth century English china. Over the next twenty years she became an authority on the subject, finally presenting it to the nation.

Towards the end of her life she took up the cause of Turkish refugees from the Balkan Wars, selling their embroideries through the big London stores (she was a good embroideress herself). Her final kindness seems the most eccentric, for she began knitting long red woollen mufflers for London cab drivers. She also built them a shelter at Langham Place, which she personally kept supplied with daily newspapers, thus helping to create one of the most articulate and opiniated sections of society in the land!

Lady Charlotte Guest died in 1895, at the age of eighty-three, and was buried in the churchyard of Canford Magna, not far from her beloved second husband.

General Pitt-Rivers (1827-1900), father of British archaeology

Born in Yorkshire and educated at Sandhurst, General Pitt-Rivers' connection with Dorset began late in life, when he inherited extensive estates at Rushmore on Cranborne Chase on the death in 1880 of his great-uncle, the last Baron Rivers, by which time Pitt-Rivers was fifty-three years old.

As a professional soldier, he had done much to improve small arms training. He had served with distinction in the Crimea, reaching the rank of Lieutenant-General in 1882. But the name he made for himself in the army was different from the one we associate with him now. He was christened Augustus Henry Lane-Fox, but it was a condition of his great-uncle's will that he assume the new identity of Pitt-Rivers.

As Lane-Fox he was already well-known in scientific circles for his interest in prehistoric cultures, and was a Fellow of The Royal Society. A heaven-sent opportunity now presented itself. The 25,000 acres he had inherited, partly in Dorset and partly in Wiltshire, are archaeologically some of the richest in the British Isles, spanning every period from the prehistoric to the medieval. He immediately set to work excavating the Bronze and Iron Age barrows in the parkland around the family home at Rushmore.

Gradually, he evolved a systematic, scientific approach to excavation which became a model for later archaeologists, recording his meticulous findings in the four volumes of *Excavations in the*

Cranborne Chase. His detailed mapping and recording of his finds won him an unrivalled reputation as an accomplished archaeologist.

He established a museum in nearby Farnham, where the public could come and view free of charge a large collection of excavated material, including agricultural implements, pottery and folk art. He also opened a pleasure park, the Larmer Tree Grounds, to which thousands of visitors came each year to enjoy the concerts and entertainments, the most anticipated being the September Sports – with the gardens brilliantly lit as evening approached.

The General died in 1900 and his ashes were interred in a black marble sarcophagus in Tollard Royal church. The Farnham Museum has since closed and its contents have passed to the British Museum. His archaeological collection was presented to Oxford University and is currently displayed in the Pitt-Rivers Museum. For many, the museum bearing his name is an essential part of a day's visit to Oxford, reminding us of his contribution to our understanding of the past.

Inspector Frederick Abbeline (1843-1929), officer in charge of the Jack the Ripper case

From August to November 1888 a series of particularly gruesome murders of prostitutes in the Whitechapel area of London caused near hysteria in the capital. The Metropolitan Police Commissioner Sir Charles Warren finally put the case in the hands of one of his most trusted detectives, Inspector Abbeline, assisted by his dogged deputy, George Godley.

These were no ordinary killings – they were more of a surgical execution, which led Abbeline to believe that 'the victim is not important, so the killer must be.' The two policemen set up an enquiry which generated huge coverage in the national press. Their methods of investigation were thorough and set standards for future patterns of psychological enquiry – indeed, Abbeline's procedures are still studied by students of criminology to this day.

Because of the mystery surrounding the case, theories have been rife, such as the 'Royal Conspiracy', which claims that the murders were committed by a fanatical cabal of Freemasons to cover up the liaisons of the Duke of Clarence, a grandson of Queen Victoria known for his loose morals and his womanising.

When questioned about the Ripper case in his retirement, Abbeline was decidedly tight-lipped about the whole affair, but he let slip that 'you'd have to look for him not at the bottom of London's society at the time, but a long way up', fuelling further the theory that the murders were the work of someone from the upper classes.

The case ended, as it began, shrouded in mystery, and has never really been closed. The story has spawned countless novels (over 150 at the latest tally), it was dramatised for television in 1988 with Michael Caine playing (to great acclaim) the role of Inspector Abbeline. It was turned into the film *From Hell* in 2001, with Abbeline portrayed as an opium addict with psychic powers – undoubtedly taking the affair yet another step further away from the truth.

In reality, Frederick Abbeline was a hard-working policeman from a humble background. He was born in Blandford in 1843, younger son of Edward and Hannah Abbeline. His father was a saddler, as well as Sheriff's Officer and Clerk of the Market, and was active in local government affairs.

Abbeline joined the Metropolitan Police in 1863, at the age of twenty. In 1888, the year of the murders, he was promoted to First Class Inspector. He finished his career as Chief Inspector and resigned in 1892 after 29 years of service. Next he worked for the Pinkerton Detective Agency as their European Agent, supervising security in the casinos at Monte Carlo, where it is said that his reputation was enough to deter would-be fraudsters.

He finally retired to Bournemouth, where he died in 1929, aged 86, at 195 Holdenhurst Road, and was buried in an unmarked grave in the Wimborne Road Cemetery. A plaque to his memory was affixed to his house, and unveiled in 2001 by Deputy Assistant Commissioner John Grieve of the Metropolitan Police in the presence of His Worship the Mayor of Bournemouth, Councillor Douglas Eyre.

No photograph of Abbeline is known to exist, but there is a line drawing of him, looking for all the world like a Victorian bank manager, which I have included in this book. In the course of his career he received 84 commendations and awards, quite possibly a record for a policeman in any force anywhere.

Lady Cornelia Guest (1847-1927), benefactress of Canford and Poole

Vivacious, beautiful, intelligent, strong-willed – such were the qualities of Lady Cornelia Henrietta Maria Guest, eldest daughter of the 7th Duke of Marlborough, sister to Randolph Churchill and aunt of Winston Churchill.

Born in 1847 at Blenheim Palace and married aged twenty-one to Ivor Guest, 1st Lord Wimborne of Canford Manor, it was Cornelia who was the 'real dynamo'. An eloquent speaker, and an advocate of temperance (she had the Canford village pub closed down, opening a coffee house in its place), Cornelia's charitable works played a central part in her married life.

Broadstone owed much if its development to the Wimbornes, and when a school was opened by Lord Wimborne in 1871, Lady Wimborne paid frequent visits to ensure that high standards were maintained. Hospitals were another interest. In 1889 she purchased a house in West Street, Poole, which was converted into the Cornelia Cottage Hospital, with fourteen beds and a convalescent wing.

Influenced by his wife, Lord Wimborne began to sell land at very low prices, from four to eight pounds a plot, so that workers could afford to buy them. In 1909, Lady Wimborne went to see Hampstead Garden City and came back advocating the advantages of the 'co-partnership' system of ownership, arranging that working men in Newtown could buy land on easy terms.

From 1906, however, when Lord Wimborne's health began to deteriorate, Lady Wimborne increasingly ran the estate on her own. She showed great business acumen, and followed the latest trends in agriculture, becoming a passionate believer in small-scale use of land, through effective horticulture and cultivation on allotments.

High on her agenda was the well-being of her estate workers. She built over a hundred homes in the area, still referred to by estate agents as 'Lady Wimborne cottages', including the two rows which face each other in the centre of Canford Magna. She kept a watchful eye on the economic climate, raising rents when times were good, but lowering them if times were hard.

Lord Wimborne died in 1914, and Lady Wimborne lived on at Canford Manor until 1922, when the house was sold and turned into Canford School. She moved to Merley House, another family property, and died in 1927. Both the Wimbornes are buried at Canford Church.

Lady Wimborne's legacy to Poole is immense. Her name lives on at Poole General Hospital, built on the site of the old Cornelia Hospital, where, today, the caring work so dear to Lady Wimborne's heart continues, in the Cornelia Nurses Home, which provides accommodation for trainee nurses, who learn about their calling at lectures in nearby Cornelia House.

Lord Baden-Powell (1857-1941), founder of the Boy Scout Movement

In 1907 twenty teenagers, two men and an orderly set up camp near the shore of Brownsea Island. The two men were General Robert Baden-Powell, hero of Mafeking, and Major Maclaren, his assistant and friend.

Baden-Powell had learned in South Africa that boys could be taught self-reliance, and he believed that the same could be applied elsewhere in the world, so that young people could have a taste of adventure and grow up healthy in mind and body. The boys came from different backgrounds, some from the privileged precincts of Eton and Harrow, others from humble elementary schools. The aim was to prove that a bond could be created, whatever the circumstances of background or birth.

Self-discipline, fair play and comradeship were the order of the day, and to this end the boys were divided into patrols, called Wolves, Ravens, Curlews and Bulls, the names reflecting, from the start, the importance of closeness to nature and respect for the environment.

In a healthy spirit of competition they learned to cook, to track, to take physical exercise and to develop powers of concentration. In the evening they sat around the camp fire, singing songs or listening to yarns about adventures in the African bush.

The fortnight's experiment was a resounding success, and the Boy Scout Movement was born. Baden-Powell came to be known simply as 'B.P.', an acronym that matched neatly the Scout motto, 'Be Prepared'. After only two years the Movement was growing rapidly, and in 1909 'B.P.' was knighted.

Little could he have realised that, in 1909, the future Lady Baden-Powell was already living in Poole, on Crichel Mount, Lilliput, in her father's large Edwardian house, 'Grey Rigg'.

Early in 1912, Olave St Clair Soames was on a cruise. Baden-Powell was also a passenger. They met at dinner at the captain's table, and despite a considerable difference in age, found that they had much in common. They became engaged soon after the cruise, and were married in St Peter's Church, Parkstone, in October. He was fifty-five; Olave was just twenty-three.

Olave became the Chief Guide as a counterpart to her husband's role as Chief Scout. They toured the world, fostering brotherhood amongst the nations, through the meeting of youth of every conceivable nationality at International Jamborees.

'B.P.' was made a peer of the realm in 1929, and awarded the Order of Merit in 1937. When he died in 1941, aged eighty-four, Olave was heart-broken, but she devoted the rest of her life to the great Scouting movement founded by her husband, which was begun on Brownsea Island and today has over 400 million members.

Sir Dan Godfrey (1868-1939),
founder of the Bournemouth Municipal (now Symphony) Orchestra

But for Sir Dan Godfrey, there would be no Bournemouth Symphony Orchestra, and Dorset would not be home to one of the world's finest orchestras.

Daniel Eyers Godfrey was the son of a well-known bandmaster. Following in his father's footsteps, the young Godfrey applied for and was given a post offered by the Mayor of Bournemouth to set up a band for the seaside town. A contract, commencing on Whit Monday 1893, was signed, and thus began Godfrey's beneficial association with the musical life of Bournemouth.

In the year that he was appointed, Godfrey initiated his first series of Symphony Concerts, and it was quickly realised that their appeal owed as much to Godfrey's personality on the rostrum as the qualities of the music.

Gradually he weaned audiences away from their traditional fare of military band music towards a diet of more serious classical items. Listeners became accustomed to hearing the great classical works, and they at first accepted, and then clamoured for more of the same. He was also determined to make Bournemouth's orchestra simply the best in the business. Part of the success in conditioning audiences to enjoy listening to good music was the quality of the performances, and Godfrey made sure that he had some of the most able performers to be found.

He also championed young British composers. Over the years he provided unparalleled opportunities for British composers not only to have their works performed, but also to conduct them.

At a memorable concert in July 1910, celebrating Bournemouth's centenary as a town, no less than six distinguished composers held the baton, including Godfrey. The others were Sir Edward Elgar, Sir Alexander Mackenzie, Sir Edward German, Sir Hubert Parry and Sir Charles Stanford. At the 1927 Easter Festival Symphony Concert Ralph Vaughan Williams conducted his Pastoral Symphony, and Dame Ethyl Smyth conducted the second performance of her Concerto for Violin, Horn and Orchestra.

In 1929 the BMO moved into its new home in the Pavilion, where broadcasting facilities brought the orchestra to a national audience and to ever wider acclaim. Armstrong Gibbs conducted the first public performance of his First Symphony in 1933, only a year before Godfrey's Winter Symphony Concerts Series came to an end with his retirement.

The statistics make impressive reading. In the space of 40 years he had conducted an astonishing 1,980 concerts, including a total number of 8,251 works, of which 1,810 were by British composers. Over half of those were new British works.

Sir Dan Godfrey's death in Bournemouth on the morning of 20 July 1939 brought to a close an extraordinary contribution to one town's music making, which had become celebrated throughout the nation. Not surprisingly, the reverberations of his influence continue to sound to this day.

He was buried at St Peter's, Bournemouth, and the service was attended by over a thousand mourners, who included the entire ensemble of the orchestra. Though eulogies abounded, it was felt that the most appropriate tribute should be a memorial concert in the Pavilion, and twelve days later this took place, calling to mind the inscription on Godfrey's gravestone: 'Music begins where words end.'

Sir Alan Cobham (1894-1973), giant of British aviation history
Although Sir Alan Cobham's contribution to aviation with the invention of in-flight refuelling has become his most enduring claim to fame (*see* 'Tarrant Rushton aerodrome' *on page 40*), from a personal point of view his greatest moment came when, on 1 October 1926, he landed on the Thames in his DH-50 float plane, ran up the steps to the Houses of Parliament and was greeted by a huge crowd of journalists and Members of Parliament.

The showmanship was really Cobham's attempt to prove a point. He believed that the future of civil aviation lay in passenger-carrying, long-haul flights. A friend had suggested he land on the Thames in a flying-boat opposite the Houses of Parliament and deliver a petition. Finally he had a brainwave. What if he terminated one of his long-distance flights on the river, when the eyes of the world – and the press above all – were already upon him?

He would announce a flight from Rochester to the Houses of Parliament, but his route (this part to be casually added) would be via Australia. The press were captivated by the idea, and the build-up was such that, when Cobham finally touched down in London, he had covered more than 27,000 miles, having started out just over three months earlier.

Cobham's reputation had been established earler in the 1920s. Africa was where he believed the greatest potential for civil aviation lay. Most of the continent was then under the British flag, yet travel to Africa, or within it, was extremely slow. This, Cobham thought, was where an aeroplane's speed would really pay off.

In November 1925 Cobham set off successfully for the Cape. The return journey, from the Cape to Cairo, took nine days and established a record. Cobham and his two passengers, his engineer and a Gaumont cinematographer, were the first people in history to complete the journey from Cape to Cairo by air.

Foreshadowing another vision of the future – 'Air Mail' – Cobham brought back personal letters, one of which was from the Earl of Athlone, Governor-General of South Africa, to his brother-in-law, King George V.

On his arrival in Britain, Cobham handed over the Earl of Athlone's letter directly to the king, unaware that within the space of a year he would be returning to Buckingham Palace to be knighted for his pioneering flight to the Houses of Parliament via Australia.

In his autobiography, Sir Alan Cobham is at pains to stress that, whatever the enthusiastic receptions he received along the way, he never felt that the adulation was for him – it was for civil aviation. He firmly believed that he stood for closer links between the scattered peoples of the nations of the Empire, and that by enabling people to meet and know one another, world-wide transport would bring them closer together.

Ralph Wightman (1901-1971), author and broadcaster

Ralph Wightman was the man who, besides William Barnes, brought the Dorset dialect to the notice of the world at large through programmes such as 'Country Magazine', 'Country Questions' and 'Farming Today'.

He achieved considerable fame in the post-war period, and made many BBC broadcasts about agriculture and rural life, all in his own inimitable way, with his instantly recognisable, rich Dorset dialect.

Born in Piddletrenthide in 1901, son of a farmer-cum-butcher, he lived in the neighbourhood all his life, ultimately in Puddletown, dying, aged 70, in Dorchester Hospital in 1971.

Books such as *Moss Green Days*, *Days on the Farm*, *The Wessex Heathland* and *Portrait of Dorset* helped confirm his reputation as a writer about the countryside, particularly his beloved Dorset.

He was frequently a guest celebrity on the panel of the hugely popular radio programme 'Any Questions?'. He once said of the area in which he lived, 'in my youth the fertile valley between Melcombe Bingham and Hilton was full of incredibly old people. The dialect was the richest in the county and the least contaminated by Devon or the New Forest.'

It was observations such as these, coupled with his down-to-earth commonsense, that endeared him to listeners and readers alike. His broadcast in the 1930s was a 10 minute talk about worms in sheep!

Wightman thrived at a time when wireless was the main means of communication. His voice was likened to 'heather honey, goose grease and just plain comic.' His broadcasts were heard in the furthest corners of the earth, and in so doing, this engaging countryman put Dorset firmly on the mid-twentieth-century world map.

Rolf Gardiner (1902-1971), champion of organic farming and founder member of the Soil Association

Rolf Gardiner, farmer and forester, had his roots in the Wessex countryside, as his forebears were West Country merchants, although his father was the distinguished Egyptologist, Sir Alan Gardiner. His own life as a forester and farmer in Dorset began in 1928, at Gore Farm, Ashmore, and five years later at neighbouring Springhead, Fontmell Magna.

But to understand the man, we have to be aware of his very personal philosophy. He was convinced that industrial civilisation would break down; that the monoliths of Russia and America would crush the spirit of European Christendom; that a new Dark Ages would sweep the land. In a sense, his forebodings were well founded, for within a decade the world was at war. But it was with no feelings of pessimism that he fought his crusade. Gardiner saw history as the unfolding of man's personal search for eternal values.

He actively supported agrarian work camps for the unemployed, and was firmly opposed to artificial farming methods, lauding the virtues of heritage and the nobility of the pre-industrial agrarian way.

In the 1930s Gardiner created the Springhead Ring, an attempt to establish a 'rural university' in which folk dance and song would be revived and celebrated in rural festivals. There is little doubt that the experience had a seminal influence on the lives of its members, not least the musicians amongst them. Among those who conducted at Ring meetings were musicians such as Sir Thomas Armstrong, John Gardner, Imogen Holst, Roger Norrington, Paul Steinitz and Rolf's son Sir John Eliot Gardiner.

In 1939 Gardiner revived Slape Mill, which lies in the rural idyll of the Brit valley below Netherbury. A tiny band of experienced flax workers were the nucleus of the original work force, but by 1942 the enterprise had grown into a fully-fledged rural industry. In *Harvest Rides in Wessex* he described a visit: 'Everyone came out to welcome us, the workers from the barns, the factory-girls, the Women's Land Army oiling the pulling-machines, the flax-pulling school-girls quartered at the mill, the office staff.

'I suddenly realised how populous Slape had become. In and around the buildings there were about a hundred men, women and children all busy with flax-processing and harvesting, where in 1939 there had been derelict walls and but two families of farm-workers.

'And this was growing into a community which I hoped would be more than just a community of production and wage-earning, but a community of craftsmanship and interest, of joy in work and mutual aid.'

Gardiner was no dreamer, regarding himself as 'a plain, practical working farmer'. Subsequently Gardiner went on to found the Dorset Federation of Young Farmers' Clubs, he became chairman of the Rural Industries Bureau (now the Council for Small Industries in Rural Areas), he was a founder member of the Soil Association and he was High Sheriff of Dorset from 1967 to 1968.

One month before his death, he was awarded the Peter Joseph Lenné Gold Medal 'for services to European Youth, and for precept and practice in Landscape Husbandry.' His address at Strasbourg is perhaps even more relevant now than when he delivered it: 'Society,' he said, 'will have to discipline itself to more selective consumption, to reliance on bare essentials, to thrift. Squandering our resources and reckless consumption lead to ultimate impoverishment and all-pervading illnesses of soils, plants, beasts and humankind . . . We must adopt a wiser style of living altogether, if we are to survive at all.'

Simon Combes (1940-2004), wildlife artist

Simon Combes was a Dorset-born wildlife artist who devoted his life to helping animals in Africa and who, in the end, paid with his life in pursuit of his career. In December 2004 Combes was returning from watching the sun set over the Rift Valley in Kenya, when he was attacked and killed by a bull buffalo.

Born in Shaftesbury, he moved to Kenya with his parents and brother at the age of five, later returning to England to train at the Royal Military Academy at Sandhurst. Once back in Kenya, he joined the King's Africa Rifles. After independence in 1963 he commanded the newly established Airborne Division of the Kenyan Army, fighting against Somali guerrillas.

He began painting while still in the army, quickly gaining a reputation for the meticulous skill with which he captured the grace, power and mystery of the wild. At first sight his astonishing technique seems to be photographic, but closer inspection of his paintings reveals backgrounds of an impressionistic quality, throwing the main subject into even greater focus.

He published two best-selling books, *An African Experience* and *Great Cats*, achieving worldwide recognition and receiving many awards, including the Society of Animal Artists' Award of Excellence.

He was not solely an artist, but an avid conservationist as well. He used his fame to further wildlife awareness, and in 2003 was appointed Kenya Representative and Project Director for the Rhino Rescue Trust. He sat on boards of several conservation organisations and raised, through his art, large sums of money for their causes.

Combes was renowned for getting perilously close to the creatures he loved to paint. He claimed to have no fear of animals despite having been chased by elephants, forced to climb a tree to escape a rhino, and been bitten by a Bengal tiger. He always said that it was mankind he feared the most. Ironically, one of his best known works is the portrait of a buffalo entitled 'Menac'.

Further Reading

Adlam, Brian, *The Book of Dorchester*, Barracuda Books, 1981

Ash, John, *Victorian Vicar, The Story of Henry Deane*, Gillingham Local History Society, 1982

Baring-Gould, S., *The Lives of the Saints*, John C. Nimmo, 1897

Begg, Paul, Fido, Martin and Skinner, Keith, *The Jack the Ripper A-Z*, Headline Book Publishing, 1996

Bennett, Alan R., *Wimborne Minster, 1992, Portrait of a Town*, Dovecote Press, 1993

Best, Andrew, *Water Springing from the Ground*, Springhead Trustees, 1972

Broadley, A. M. and Bartelot, R. G., *The Three Dorset Captains at Trafalgar*, John Murray, 1906, republished with an introduction by Maureen Attwooll, Dovecote Press, 2005

Cameron, Dugald, *Glasgow's Own*, Squadron Prints, 1987

Chandler, James, *Great Characters in Dorset*, The Book Guild, 1991

Cobham, Sir Alan J., *A Time to Fly*, Shepheard-Walwyn, 1978

Coffin, Leslie, W., *William Henry Fox Talbot*, published by Miss S. E. M. Coffin, 1996

Cooper, Allan T. P., *Benjamin Jesty, The Pre-Jennerian Vaccinator*, Dorset Natural History and Archaeological Society, 1969

Cox, Barry, *Lifeboat Gallantry, The Complete Record of Royal National Lifeboat Institution Gallantry Medals and how they were won, 1824-1996*, Spink and Son Ltd, 1998

Cox, Benjamin C., *Blandford Forum, A Pictorial History*, Phillimore, 1995
The Book of Blandford Forum, Barracuda Books, 1983

Edwards, Elizabeth, *Famous Women of Dorset*, Power Publications, no date of publication

Evans, Roger, *Somerset's Forgotten Heroes*, Dovecote Press, 2004

Hall, Ruth, *Marie Stopes*, Andre Deutsch, 1977

Hathaway, Eileen, *A Dorset Soldier, The Autobiography of Sgt William Lawrence*, Spellmount, 1993

Hinchy, F. S., *North-East Dorset, Towns and Downs*, The Dorset Bookshop, 1957
The Heart of Dorset, Blackmore Press, no date of publication

Kerr, Barbara, *Bound to the Soil*, John Baker, 1968

Lees, Dodo, *Dodo by Dodo Lees*, ed. Clive Murphy, Self Publishing Association, 1993

Legg, Rodney, *Dorset Families*, Dorset Books, 2002

    Dorset Flight, The Complete History, Dorset Publishing Company, 2001

    Literary Dorset, Dorset Publishing Company, 1990

Lloyd, Stephen, *Sir Dan Godfrey*, Thames Publishing, 1995

Lonsdale, Jeremy, *The Army's Grace*, Spellmount, 1992

Maxwell, Donald, *Unknown Dorset*, John Lane: The Bodley Head, 1927

Mee, Arthur, *Dorset (The King's England Series)*, Hodder & Stoughton, 1939

Monk, Murial, *10,000 Fallen Remembered on Dorset War Memorials*, Somerset and Dorset Family History Society, 2000

National Maritime Museum, *Treasures of the National Maritime Museum*, NMM, 2004

Osborn, George, *Dorset Curiosities*, Dovecote Press, 1986

Pead, Patrick J., *Benjamin Jesty: new light in the dawn of vaccination*, The Lancet, 2003

Pillinger, Colin, *Beagle*, Faber & Faber, 2003

Sampson, R. W. F. with Norman Franks, *Spitfire Offensive*, Grub Street, 1994

Shores, Christopher, *Aces High*, Grub Street, 1994

    Aces High, Volume 2, Grub Street, 1999

Stokes, Doug, *Paddy Finucane: Fighter Ace*, William Kimber, 1983

Thomas, Gil, *Shoulder The Sky*, Arthur Barker Limited, 1959

Trenchard, Diana, *Women of Dorset*, Dorset Books, 1994

TUC General Council, *The Book of The Martyrs of Tolpuddle*, Pelican Press, 1934

Wallace, E. Marjorie, MA, *The First Vaccinator*, published privately, no date

Ward, Peter, *Came Down to Golf!*, Ellesborough Press, 1984

Whitcombe, R. A., *Golf's No Mystery!*, J. M. Dent and Sons, 1938

Williams, Peter and Harrison, Ted, *McIndoe's Army*, Pelham Books, 1979

Index

Plate page numbers are shown in **bold**

St Jude, Milton 100; St John sub Castro, Lewes 103; Canford Magna 105; St Peter's, Parkstone 110

Churchill, Randolph 108

Churchill, Winston 35, 39, 108

Civil War, English 53-57, 74, 75

Clairet, Clotilde 25

Clarence, Duke of 106

Clubmen, The 56

Cobham, Sir Alan 41, 112, 113, **pl 23**

Coe, Chris 52

Coke, Lady Jane Elizabeth 23

Colchester 74

Colmar Gap 37

Combes, Simon 115, **pl 24**

Combination Laws, Repeal of (1824) 59

Corfe Castle 54, 55, 92

Corscombe 97

Counter, Jack Thomas 15, **pl 3**

Courtrai 13

Cowes 86

Cowpox 77, 78

Coxon, Elizabeth 80

Cranborne Chase 40, 56, 105, 106

Crawley New Town 34

Cricket: Jeremy Lonsdale (biographer of R. M. Poore) 62; Don Bradman 62; Somerset 62; Hampshire 62, 63; County Championship 63; Ranston League 63; Bournemouth Cricket and Sports Club 63; Gentlemen of Dorset 63; Cricketer's Arms, Holdenhurst Rd, Bournemouth 68

Cromwell, Oliver 56, 94

Cross, Violet Norah 26, **pl 5**

Cross-Channel Swimming: Sam Rockett 69, 70; *Daily Mail* International Channel Race 69; Godfrey Chapman 70; Antonio Abertondo 70; Samantha Druce 70

Crozier, Mount 61

Dachau 37

Dad's Army 70

Dagnall, Tom **pl 10**

Damory Court 55

Danube, R. 37

Dargai Heights 11

Dartmouth 71

Darwin, Charles 82

Davies, Lt George, RN 46

D-Day, 29, 32, 33, 35, 37, 40, 42, 53

Deane, Henry 99, **pl 18**

Deelfontein 86

Delhi 10

Deloge, Henri 64

Descartes, René 76

Devon 90, 93, 113

Dieppe 32

Digby, Admiral Sir Robert 22

Digby, Henry 22, **pl 4**

Digby, Lady, of Sherborne 54

Disraeli, Benjamin 103

Dolphin pub, Kinson 64

Dorchester 59, 84, 85, 94

Dorchester Hospital 85, 113

Dorset County Council 28, 38

Dorset Federation of Young Farmers Clubs 115

Doulting 93

Dover 70

Dowlais Iron Works 104

Downshay Farm 78

Driver, Private Lionel 40

Duncliffe Hill 56

Dunham, Sir Kingsley 89

Dunkirk 46

Durham University 84, 89

Durweston 102, 103

Dwyer, Leslie 70

East End, London 86

East Grinstead 33, 34

East Stour 100

Echo newspaper 42

Edinburgh 87

Edwara, Saint 91

Edward VII 83-85

Egypt 70

Elgar, Sir Edward 111

English Channel 13, 50, 69, 70

Enmore Green 99

Entertainments National Services Association (ENSA) 42

Epinoy 16

Eros Films 70

Eros Statue (Piccadilly Circus) 102

Eton College 109

Exeter 46, 47, 53, 95

Exmouth 49

Eyre, Cllr Douglas, Mayor of Bournemouth 107

Factory Act (1833) 101

Fairfax, General 56, 57

Farnham 106

Farren, Major Roy (SAS) 39

Fédération Aéronautique Internationale (FAI) 66

Ferguson, Alasdair 32, **pl 6**
Finucane, Paddy 29
First Aid Nursing Yeomanry (FANY) 39
Flanders 39
Flann, William 46
Fleet Air Arm 30, 31
Folkestone 70
Fontmell Magna 10
Football: Wimborne Town Football Club
    72, 73, **pl 13**; Jewson Wessex League 72;
    Dorset Senior Cup 72; Wembley Stadium
    72, 73; FA Vase 72, 73; Premiership
    League 72; Championship League 72;
    First & Second Divisions 72;
    Mangotsfield FC 72; Chard Town FC
    72; Horsham FC 72; Hastings Town FC
    73; Newcastle Town FC 73; Diss Town
    FC 73; Bamber Bridge FC 73; Guiseley
    FC 73
Fordington 98
Forres Preparatory School 71
Fort George 14
Fort Rioux 21
Fox Talbot, William Henry 6
FR Group plc (formerly Flight Refuelling
    Limited) 41
Freemasons 106
Fremantle, Commander Charles Howe RN
    45
Fremantle, Western Australia 46
Friendly Society of Agricultural Labourers
    59
Fripp, Sir Alfred Downing 85
Frome, R. 58
Fuggle, Jean 34

Gabard, E. 65
Galilei, Galileo 76
Gallipoli 39
Gardiner, Rolf 114, **pl 24**
Gardiner, Sir Alan 114
Gardiner, Sir John Eliot 114
Gardner, John 114
Gates, Reginald 87
Geological Society 79
George II 96
George III 22
George V 15, 66, 84, 85, 112
German, Sir Edward 110
Gibbs, Armstrong 110
Gibraltar 35, 98
Gillingham 99
Glasgow 25

Glisson, Francis 74
Gloucestershire 86
Godfrey, Sir Dan 110, **pl 21**
Godley, George 106
Godolphin, Baron 102
Gold Beach 33
Golden Gate Bridge 13
Golf: Broadstone Golf Club 63, 64;
    Ranelagh Club 63; Sandwich 63, 67;
    Dorset Golf Club 63; Cavalry Club 63;
    Dorset Amateurs 63; English Senior
    Golfers Society 63; Captain A. V.
    Hambro, MP 64; Dorset Amateur Golf
    Championship 64; Reginald (R.A.)
    Whitcombe 67, **pl 11**; Open
    Championship 67; Westward Ho! 67;
    J. H. Taylor 67; Ernest Whitcombe 67;
    Charles Whitcombe 67; Came Down 67,
    68; Western Counties Championship 67;
    Ryder Cup 67; Henry Cotton 67;
    Carnoustie 67; Parkstone Golf Club 68
Gore Farm 114
Gott, Susannah 81
Gould, John 80, 81, **pl 15**
Grand National Consolidated Trades
    Union 59
Greenwich 11, 22
Greenwich Hospital 20
Grieve, John, Dep Asst Commissioner
    Metropolitan Police 107
Grosvenor family 99
Guest, Cornelia, Lady Wimborne 108
Guest, Ivor, Lord Wimborne 104, 108
Guest, Lady Charlotte 103, **pl 20**
Guest, Sir John 104
Guinea Pig Club 33
Gulliver's Tavern 64
Guy's Hospital 85, 86

Halifax, Canada 21
Hall, Captain Ronald 40
Hall, Ed 99
Halstock 91, 97
Hambledon Hill 57
Hamilton, Duke of 63
Hammett, James 59
Hampshire 22, 62, 63, 66
Hampstead Garden City 108
Hamworthy Engineering 33
Hansford, John 46
Hardy Memorial 20
Hardy, Ronald James 49
Hardy, Thomas 6, 85